OTHER BOOKS BY LINDA MERINOFF

THE GLORIOUS NOODLE

THE SAVORY SAUSAGE

# GINGERBREAD

NINETY-NINE DELICIOUS

RECIPES FROM SWEET TO SAVORY

# LINDA MERINOFF

A FIRESIDE BOOK PUBLISHED BY SIMON & SCHUSTER INC.

NEW YORK    LONDON    TORONTO    SYDNEY    TOKYO

FIRESIDE
SIMON & SCHUSTER BUILDING
ROCKEFELLER CENTER
1230 AVENUE OF THE AMERICAS
NEW YORK, NEW YORK 10020

DESIGNED BY BONNI LEON
MANUFACTURED IN THE UNITED STATES OF AMERICA

10   9   8   7   6   5   4   3   2

LIBRARY OF CONGRESS CATALOGING-IN-PUBLICATION DATA
MERINOFF, LINDA.
    GINGERBREAD/LINDA MERINOFF.
        P.   CM.
    "A FIRESIDE BOOK."
    INCLUDES BIBLIOGRAPHICAL REFERENCES.
    1. GINGERBREAD.   I. TITLE.
TX771.M39   1989
641.8'653—DC20                                        89-37558
                                                        CIP

ISBN 0-671-67293-2

# ACKNOWLEDGMENTS

I'd like to begin by thanking the people who directly led to this book. Eileen Stukane, a close friend and the only person I trust to write a "Healthy Eating" column without succumbing to quackery and faddism, recommended me to *Food & Wine* magazine. Working with Warren Picower, Tina Ujlaki, Stanley Dry, and everyone else at the magazine is like being transported back to a perhaps mythical time when courtesy, gentle good humor, and the appreciation of the written word were all equally important. My second *Food & Wine* article was on gingerbread, and soon after, Sydny Miner asked me to write this book.

Several others contributed to the book in a direct or peripheral fashion. I would have found it impossible to become a full-time writer without the loving support of Herman, Susan, Charlie, Leigh, Spencer, and Barbara Merinoff, and Cathy and Bill Onufrychuk. Cathy is also the reason I have to resist laughing out loud every time I smell gingerbread baking, but that's another story. Cindy Cable and Jay Kulli gave me my first Cushion-Aire baking sheet, which turned me into a confident baker.

My desire to write about food was enhanced by the work of several food-writing pastmasters. Craig Claiborne and Julia Child were my earliest inspirations, followed by M. F. K. Fisher and Calvin Trillin. The writing of Mr. Claiborne and Mrs. Child made me realize that simple, beautifully prepared food can and should be part of our everyday lives. Mr. Claiborne, through his *New York Times* articles, first introduced me (and many other Americans) to many of the exciting and exotic cuisines I now, lovingly, take for granted—Thai, Indonesian, Persian, Mexican, and Brazilian, to name just a few. Mrs. Fisher, who evokes more magic and romance writing about a Burgundian restaurant's little baked onions than is found in a thousand Harlequin novels, demonstrates how soaring food writing can be, while Mr. Trillin brings it crashing down to earth with bemused, often silly, wonderful tales of tamales and fries and adventures with Suds and Dregs.

Five authors especially influenced this particular book. Mrs. Rombauer and Mrs. Becker's *Joy of Cooking* is a constant source of basic kitchen information. Edward Espe Brown's *Tassajara Bread Book* taught me how to unfailingly, easily, and joyfully bake perfect bread. Mimi Sheraton's *German Cookbook* and Nika Hazelton's German, American, and Belgian cookbooks were all clear, fascinating, definitive research sources.

Final thanks go to two of the most important people in my life. Larry Strichman is my best critic, cheerleader, and fellow adventurer. Paul Bogrow is just about everything else. It's inconceivable to me that I could accomplish anything without them.

This book is dedicated to the striking-looking, funny, inspiring, supportive, intellectually challenging Sydny Miner . . . and to Brian (my favorite baking assistant), Jacob, and Zachary Onufrychuk and Leslie Merinoff, my nephews and niece, who are the reason I keep trying to build a bigger and better gingerbread house.

# CONTENTS

**INTRODUCTION** 9

**A BRIEF HISTORY OF GINGERBREAD** 16

**DESSERTS** 19

**BREADS, MUFFINS, AND BREAKFASTS** 109

**SAVORY DISHES** 139

**THE CHRISTMAS SEASON CALENDAR** 161

**MAIL ORDER SOURCES** 178

**BIBLIOGRAPHY** 183

**INDEX** 187

**I**f global unity depends upon the realization of what we all have in common, then gingerbread may hold the key to world peace. Well, that might be a *bit* of an exaggeration, but I can't think of any other food that brings a smile to the face of everyone but the most stiff-necked Scrooge. From Russia to Jamaica, Austria to Indonesia, Scandinavia to South Africa, gingerbread is universally loved. Close your eyes and remember that provocative spicy smell, that delicious taste so familiar and yet so exotic, those happy occasions on which you've shared it with friends and family. It's impossible to be unhappy while biting the hump off a camel-shaped cookie or wiping the cake's whipped cream topping off your mustache.

It seems appropriate to begin by defining the subject. For the purpose of this book, gingerbread is a cookie, cake, pastry, or bread in which the taste of ginger is distinctive. Oddly enough, some gingerbreads have no ginger and few are breads. Frequently "gingerbread" actually refers to any kind of spice cake, whether it includes ginger or not; the taste many people assume is ginger is actually molasses. I've included only real gingerbreads, which means that, much to my regret, excellent recipes such as the French pain d'épices and many of the German molded cookies aren't here.

As to the "bread," *all* early baked goods were made from bread doughs. Sweeteners were expensive, leavening agents undependable, and kitchen fires too unpredictable to produce anything as delicate as a modern cake. Even in Victorian times, gingerbread was usually relegated to breakfast or afternoon tea; only in the last sixty years has it become almost exclusively a dessert. It's still denser and often coarser than most other cakes, which may be what makes it so utterly satisfying.

There are traditional recipes in this book, some familiar, others somewhat less well-known. Most of us have tasted the basic gingerbread cookies and cake, Swedish and American gingersnaps, and German sauerbraten with gingersnap sauce. But the amazing Dutch-Indonesian "bacon cake," in which cocoa-gingerbread layers alternate with white cake, and British parkin, an oatmeal ginger cake, for example, may be new to most Americans.

Other recipes in the book were created by judiciously adding gingerbread flavorings to usually blander items. A marble cake in which gingerbread and cheesecake are swirled, peanut butter cookies with butterscotch chips, a white chocolate torte, savory onion-walnut quick bread, gingerbread cannolis with candied ginger ricotta filling, gingersnap-coated potato croquettes, and custardy pecan pie with a gingersnap crust are just a few of my favorites.

In researching gingerbread, I've discovered some wonderful rationalizations for eating it. From the fourteenth century on, ginger was (and sometimes still is) believed to soothe troubled stomachs. In 1987, medical magazines reported on lab studies using ground ginger—filled capsules. One study showed that ginger produces an anticlotting effect similar to that of aspirin. Two other studies claim ginger is more effective than current popular medications in preventing motion sickness. Having no medical background, I don't know if any of these studies are valid. I'm sure you'd also require a lot more ginger than you get in one piece of gingerbread for it to work. Still, it's nice to know that, occasionally, good food may just be good for you.

Since I've tried not only to provide recipes but also to inspire you to create your own, the following is a guide to the equipment and ingredients used in baking gingerbread.

## BAKING EQUIPMENT

Baking is quicker, more efficient, and a lot easier if you have the correct equipment. All the items below are available at good cookware or hardware stores, and I strongly recommend them. For information on more specific equipment, including the various cake pans, check individual recipes.

**BAKING SHEET**     Since I discovered the Cushion-Aire baking sheet, composed of two sheets of aluminum with air trapped between them, I haven't burned anything. They come in two sizes, so choose the correct one; you must have at least one inch of clearance between the edges of the sheet and the walls and door of your oven or your food won't cook evenly. You can buy them in most department-store housewares departments, or they can be mail-ordered from the sources listed in the back of the book (see "Mail Order Sources" chapter).

**CAKE TESTER**     Specialized sterling silver testers, toothpicks, clean broom straws, and small wooden skewers work equally well. Insert the tester into the center of a cake; if there's no batter on it when it's withdrawn, the cake is done.

**COOKIE MOLDS AND STAMPS**     See "Christmas Season Calendar" and "Mail Order Sources" chapters.

**CUTTING AND PASTRY BOARD**     I find that a good, sturdy acrylic board, such as Joyce Chen's, is more easily cleaned than wood. Make sure the board can't be marred by knives, or dirt will get trapped in the scratches and the board will smell terrible.

**PAM AND BAKERS JOY**     These sprays make greasing (Pam) or greasing and flouring (Bakers Joy) a pan or baking sheet absolutely effortless.

**PARCHMENT PAPER**    Now often found in supermarkets, it prevents baked goods from sticking to the pan or baking sheet. It's also helpful if you don't have enough baking sheets; just slide the paper with the baked cookies off the sheet and slide a fresh paper with unbaked cookies on. Substitute waxed paper in cake pans, and foil on baking sheets.

**ROLLING PIN**    It should be straight, not tapered at the ends.

**THERMOMETERS**    An accurate deep-frying thermometer takes the guesswork out of both frying and candy-making. An oven thermometer helps you compensate for an uneven oven or faulty thermostat.

**WIRE COOLING RACKS**    Round, square, or rectangular, they ensure that baked goods will cool evenly and prevent soggy undersides, since air circulates below them. A wire pasta rack can also be used.

## GINGERBREAD INGREDIENTS

I can't stress too much how important it is to use the best possible raw ingredients in cooking, since the finished product can be no better than its components. With gingerbread, however, you have a wide range of possibilities. No matter which combination of flour, sweetener, fat, liquid, spices, and other flavorings you use, you're probably replicating a gingerbread already popular somewhere in the world.

**SPICES**    Ginger is sold fresh, ground, crystallized (candied), and pickled; the first three are used in baking. The best, palest, most delicate ginger available in America usually specifies that it's Jamaican on the bottle. Cheaper, darker gingers can be harsh. One tablespoon of minced fresh ginger is the equivalent of one-eighth to one-quarter teaspoon of ground. Ginger juice is often used in Caribbean cakes, beverages, soups, and jellies. Just simmer any amount of finely chopped or crushed fresh ginger in water to cover until the water is reduced by half. Strain and store in the refrigerator. To use, replace ¼ cup liquid in a cake recipe with that amount of ginger juice and omit the ground ginger.

Many gingerbreads contain equal amounts of ginger and either cinnamon or cloves plus smaller amounts of two or three other ground spices. Cinnamon mellows the ginger, while cloves add more intensity. Americans usually add allspice and nutmeg, Scandinavians cardamom. Ground mace or coriander and whole aniseed or caraway seeds are other possibilities.

**FLOURS**　　All of the following flours can be found in supermarkets. White and unbleached flours work equally well and are indistinguishable in the final product, so use whichever you prefer. Cake flour is made from softer wheat, so cakes are crumbly rather than elastic like bread. Substitute one cup minus two tablespoons of unbleached or white flour for one cup of cake flour if necessary.

The rougher taste of whole wheat flour stands up to ginger in bread recipes. Its texture, however, is very dense, so use half whole wheat and half white or unbleached flour. Graham flour is just another name for whole wheat. Rye flour, used in European gingerbreads, makes a sticky, more dense, strong-tasting cake. Rice flour and cornstarch, which are so fine they're powdery, can be used in delicate cookies such as shortbread. For oatmeal desserts, I use rolled oats in cookies and very thin cakes, finer oatmeal in regular cakes. Unprocessed wheat bran is best for baking. Ground almonds, hazelnuts, or walnuts replace almost all the flour in tortes—rich, thin cakes usually served without frosting.

**SWEETENERS**　　With all their distinctive differences, they are as important to the taste and texture of gingerbread as the spices. Molasses and honey not only add flavor, they also help baked goods stay fresh longer. I prefer unsulfured molasses to the other types; sulfured and blackstrap are too strong. Regional favorites are sometimes substituted for molasses. In the American South, cane and sorghum syrups are popular, while Britons use black treacle or the milder golden syrup.

Honey is the most important ingredient in German lebkuchen, and it's often aged at least a year before it's used. The earliest gingerbreads were made with honey, since sugar was unavailable or exorbitantly expensive. Good honey mellows gingerbread, smoothing out any harsh spicing. Light corn syrup adds only sweetness to a recipe, while dark corn syrup has a slightly more distinctive taste.

Brown sugar is white sugar which hasn't been purged of all its molasses. Using the light or dark version of molasses, honey, corn syrup, or brown sugar is purely a matter of personal taste. Choose whichever you like best unless one kind is specified in a recipe. Regular white and superfine sugar can be used interchangeably. I prefer superfine or the similar English castor sugar for meringues and macaroons.

**FATS**    These tenderize and add flavor and color to gingerbread. Animal fats—British mutton fat, American salt pork, and internationally available lard—all seem to melt away, leaving delicious and tender pastry. Bacon fat makes a wonderful dark gingerbread cake. Vegetable shortening is adequate. I usually cook with butter because I love the taste, and I prefer unsalted since it's usually fresher; I can always add salt to the recipe if I choose.

**LEAVENING AGENTS**    I use double-acting baking powder, since that's what's most commonly found in supermarkets. Baking soda leavens and tenderizes those recipes with acidic ingredients, such as lemon juice, vinegar, buttermilk, or molasses. Too much baking soda leaves a terrible metallic taste, so small amounts are often used along with baking powder.

Powdered hartshorn, which is exactly what it sounds like, was once used to make cookies very crispy. Ammonium carbonate, the modern equivalent, is still used in northern Europe. Sometimes sold in small lumps in American drugstores, it is easily crushed before using. You can also order it from Maid of Scandinavia (see page 180). Use the same amount as you would baking powder or soda.

Eggs are often the only leavening agent in delicate cakes, since the taste of baking soda or powder can be too harsh. For lighter cakes, whip the egg whites until stiff, then gently fold in without deflating them. Whipped cream serves the same purpose. If you add eggs or cream to a recipe, decrease other fats. For yeast information, see individual recipes in the bread chapter.

**LIQUIDS** You can use almost any liquid in gingerbread. Dairy products—sweet, evaporated, or sour milk; buttermilk; fresh or sour cream; and yogurt—produce rich cakes. Ale or beer (often used in parkin), West Indian coconut milk, and fresh fruit juice each add their own distinctive flavor.

**FLAVORINGS** The trick is to use enough flavoring to emerge from and complement the ginger without overwhelming it. Try rum, brandy, or cognac; liqueurs (especially orange or nut); cocoa or chocolate; coffee; grated lemon or orange rind; or pure lemon, vanilla, or almond extract. If you're not sure how much to use, add the flavoring last, a little at a time, tasting the batter or dough constantly.

**VEGETABLE AND FRUIT PUREES** See pages 49, 53, 58, 111, and 126.

Though commonplace today, ginger and gingerbread were once considered as valuable as precious gems. Thousands of years ago when the spice trade began, men, animals, and ships perished in their quest to trade Asian spices for European and Middle Eastern riches. While Phoenician and Arab traders first carried ginger from Southeast Asia, it was the Romans who spread spices throughout Europe. Great, almost fanatical lovers of exotic foods, the Romans demanded spiced food whether they were at home or in their colonies such as Germany, France, or Britain. Some historians believe that the first gingered breads were created by the Egyptians, Greeks, and Romans, who either baked honey in the breads or spread it on top.

After Rome fell, spices disappeared from Europe for hundreds of years. When the Portuguese, Dutch, British, and French began fighting for the rights to the lucrative Asian spice trade, breads made with the very expensive ginger became a status symbol. As sugar and other cane products such as molasses were even scarcer than ginger, local honeys were always used as sweeteners.

The medieval version of gingerbread would be unrecognizable today. Bread crumbs tossed with honey and spices were dried out or baked into hard, crumbly, flat cakes. Some of the cakes were pressed into molds to form beautiful and elaborate pictures. Gingerbread men, called gingerbread husbands, became popular in northern Britain. Considered a gift fit for or from a king, or an appropriate ending to a great banquet, huge slabs of gingerbread were gilded with real gold and studded decoratively with gold-dipped cloves. Dark gingerbreads got their reddish-brown color from sandalwood or red wine, while white gingerbread was actually ginger-flavored marzipan.

By the end of the Middle Ages, gingerbread had greatly evolved. Cakes similar to today's cookies had made their debut to great acclaim and were just inexpensive enough for common folk to afford on special occasions—ungilded, of course. Gingerbread vendors were often the most popular attraction at medieval fairs. Sandalwood and red wine had given way first to licorice, then to molasses (called treacle in England). In the late sixteenth century, Queen Elizabeth I employed a full-time gingerbread baker. Some of the old gingerbread molds are still used today in Queen Elizabeth II's kitchens.

The beginning of Europe's relationship with its neighbors across the Atlantic made gingerbread accessible to everyone. Imported sugarcane and spice plants thrived in the Caribbean, bringing prices down. Hard gingerbreads were joined by the more delicate cakes in the eighteenth and nineteenth centuries. The cakes were often toasted and eaten for breakfast or served with coffee or tea. Both cakes and cookies became American favorites, especially in Louisiana, where molasses was produced, and in New England. The hardest gingerbreads, Louisiana's molasses-laden *estomac mulâtre* (mulatto's stomach) and New England's glazed muster gingerbread, were especially valued since they could be kept for weeks without spoiling. In her lifetime, Emily Dickinson was praised as much for her gingerbread as for her poetry. Most modern cookies and cakes were developed in the late nineteenth and early twentieth centuries, and all today's recipes are merely variations on those.

# DESSERTS

**T**he smell of baking spice cookies permeates almost every country in the world, and those cookies with ginger are the most popular of all. Nowadays, delicious ginger cookies are too often exclusive to Christmas, which is truly a waste. While that may be because many of them are molded or cut into or printed with extraordinary pictures, there are also simple cookies appropriate for every day. What could be better than a gingersnap that's both chewy and crispy at the same time? Or a hard-but-not-too-hard gingerbread cookie in the shape of a camel or groundhog or George Washington's head, depending on your whim and the cookie cutters in your collection? Not to mention the comforting, mouth-watering aroma that makes every house smell like Grandma's.

European gingerbread cookies are wonderful both to eat and to see. Lithuanian grybai appear to be mushrooms, while the crunchy texture of Tyrolean rye flour and grated hazelnut cookies is unbeatable. Scandinavian scalloped round cookies, rolled into fancier shapes at Christmas, are distinguished by cardamom and sometimes orange peel. It would be unthinkable not to mention The Netherlands' almond and candied ginger delights; our word "cookies" comes from their *koekjes*, which means "little cakes."

While many cities call themselves the gingerbead capital of the world, Nürnberg, West Germany, has a good claim on the title. In a honey-producing area and once the center of spice trading routes, it is the home of the justifiably famous lebkuchen (honey gingerbread). The record for greatest gingerbread variety must be held by Britain, with its oatmeal parkin; several kinds of brandy snaps, including orange-flower water–flavored Hampshire Mothering Sunday wafers; Shah biscuits with candied citron; and ginger macaroons—to name just a few.

Gingerbread spread around the world from Europe, and local ingredients and recipes create some interesting variations. Crude molasses gives Guatemalan cookies a distinctive taste. One Caribbean restaurant sandwiches gingersnaps with whipped cream into a long roll similar to the American icebox cake. Moravians, Czechoslovakian immigrants who settled in both the Caribbean and eastern United States, brought delicious, crisp, very, very thin ginger cookies with them. South African cookies are made with grape syrup. And in the Middle East, gingerbread squares include walnuts, almonds, and pistachios.

American cookies are often called crinkles, hermits, gingersnaps, ginger nuts, boiled cookies, or just molasses cookies. My favorite name is Joe Froggers, a rum-and-molasses New England cookie. Legend has it that they were created in the nineteenth century by an old man named Joe with a fondness for rum; the large cookies looked like frogs.

The way a cookie is formed depends upon the stiffness of the dough. The firmest dough can be rolled out and cut with a knife or cookie cutters, or pressed into molds. Slightly softer but still fairly firm dough is rolled into a ball, then lightly squashed into rounds, or is formed into logs, refrigerated, then cut into thin slices. When the dough is soft, dollops are dropped from a spoon onto the baking sheet. Batters are poured in rectangular pans, then cut into bars when baked, or they're dropped into molds to form cakelike cookies.

The basic proportion I start with when creating any ginger cookie is 1¼ to 1½ teaspoons spice for every cup of flour. I usually use equal amounts of ginger and either cinnamon or cloves and add a small amount of allspice, nutmeg, and/or cardamom. Then I keep tasting the dough. When it's slightly spicier than I think the cookies should be, it's perfect. The spiciness mellows out slightly in the cooking. Let your common sense be your guide. If there are other dry ingredients along with the flour—such as oatmeal, for example—add that amount to the flour when you're calculating how much spice to use.

While most of the recipes below are not for traditional gingerbread cookies, they are all wonderful with gingerbread spices and molasses, honey, and/or brown sugar in them. There are a few general techniques to remember when making cookies.

If there's a large proportion of sugar the cookies will be chewy. To mold cookies into shapes such as tuiles, fortune cookies, or brandy snaps, use lots of sugar and butter and be sure to shape them as soon as they come out of the oven, before they lose their flexibility.

When making a stiff cookie dough that is to be rolled out, use just as much flour as is necessary to prevent it from sticking to the board and your rolling pin. If you use too much flour, the cookies will be hard and dry. If necessary, dip your cookie cutters in flour before cutting out the cookies.

To make soft cookies, bake them a few minutes less than you would to make hard ones.

If a recipe says to grease and flour a baking sheet, rather than just to grease it, that's important. The flour stops cookies from spreading too much and running into each other.

If you store your cookies in an airtight container, they'll keep for at least a week and often longer. To freeze cookies, place them, not touching and on a greased baking sheet, in the freezer. Then store the frozen cookies in a sealed plastic bag. That way you can remove only as many as you need.

Please note that the Swedish molded cookie pepparkakor is covered in "The Christmas Season Calendar" chapter.

This is the traditional gingerbread cookie dough; it can be shaped into simple gingerbread men, fearsome dinosaurs, even elaborate Victorian mansions. Since the dough can be stored for two weeks in the refrigerator, and the cookies will keep for at least a month in an airtight container, there's no excuse not to have them around. It's also such a sturdy dough that children can roll and reroll it repeatedly and the cookies will still taste delicious.

| | |
|---|---|
| 2½ TEASPOONS GROUND GINGER | ½ CUP UNSALTED BUTTER |
| 1¼ TEASPOONS GROUND CINNAMON | ¾ CUP MOLASSES |
| ½ TEASPOON GROUND CARDAMOM | ½ CUP WHITE SUGAR |
| ½ TEASPOON GROUND NUTMEG | 2 TABLESPOONS WATER |
| ¼ TEASPOON GROUND CLOVES | 1 LARGE EGG |
| ½ TEASPOON BAKING SODA | 3 CUPS UNBLEACHED OR WHITE |
| ¼ TEASPOON SALT | PRESIFTED ALL-PURPOSE FLOUR |

Mix together the ginger, cinnamon, cardamom, nutmeg, cloves, baking soda, and salt and set aside.

Melt the butter in a small saucepan. Remove from the heat and stir in the molasses and sugar. Beat in the spice mixture completely, then the water, then the egg.

Place the flour in a large bowl and make a large well in the center. Pour the butter mixture into the well. Stir about a quarter of the flour, the part closest to the center, into the molasses mixture. Stir in half the remaining flour, then the rest. When all the flour has been incorporated, turn the dough out onto a board and knead just until smooth. Roll the dough into a ball, wrap in plastic, and refrigerate overnight or up to 2 weeks.

When you're ready to bake your cookies, preheat the oven to 350°F. and grease the baking sheets. Roll out some of the dough ⅛″ thick, keeping the rest well wrapped in plastic. Cut into shapes with a 5″ cookie cutter. Bake the cookies on the sheets for 12 minutes. Remove from the oven, gently lift off the cookies with a spatula, and cool them on a rack. Make the rest of the cookies the same way. Decorate the cooled gingerbread or leave plain.

**MAKES ABOUT 80 MEDIUM-SIZE COOKIES**

A British favorite for hundreds of years, these are now so popular in ex-colonies such as the United States that we feel they're typically all-American. The main difference between snaps and rolled cookies is that these have a greater proportion of sugar, which is what makes them chewy or brittle, depending on how long they're baked. In England, they're sometimes rolled around a spoon handle while hot, then filled with whipped cream just before serving.

If you have only two baking sheets, cover them with foil or parchment before you drop on the cookies. Slide the foil with baked cookies off the sheet and slide on another piece covered with unbaked cookies.

| | |
|---|---|
| 1 TEASPOON GROUND GINGER | 2 TABLESPOONS LIGHT CORN SYRUP |
| 1 TEASPOON GROUND CLOVES | 1 LARGE EGG |
| ½ TEASPOON GROUND CINNAMON | 1 TEASPOON WHITE VINEGAR |
| 1 TEASPOON BAKING SODA | 1 CUP WHITE SUGAR |
| ½ CUP UNSALTED BUTTER, AT ROOM TEMPERATURE | 2 CUPS UNBLEACHED OR WHITE PRESIFTED ALL-PURPOSE FLOUR |
| 2 TABLESPOONS MOLASSES | |

Mix together the ginger, cloves, cinnamon, and baking soda and set aside. Preheat the oven to 325°F. Beat the butter, molasses, and corn syrup until smooth. Beat in the egg, vinegar, spice mixture, sugar, and flour, in that order.

Using damp hands, roll the dough into 1"-diameter balls. Place about 1" apart on ungreased baking sheets. Slightly flatten the balls with the wet tines of a fork. Then gently press again, with the tines at right angles to the marks already on the cookies, to flatten them until they're about ½" high. The crisscross pattern on top of the cookies gives them their traditional crinkly top. Bake for 15 minutes for chewy cookies, 18 minutes if you prefer them crisper.

Remove the baking sheets from the oven and let the cookies cool in place for 3 to 4 minutes. Then carefully move with a spatula to a cooling rack. Eat warm or at room temperature.

**MAKES 70 COOKIES**

There's something irresistible about the texture of oatmeal cookies. You feel real satisfaction, unlike the transient pleasure of feather-light cookies or lingering unctuousness of rich butter cookies. Ginger seems to have a warming effect, so these are a perfect winter cookie.

| | |
|---|---|
| ½ CUP UNSALTED BUTTER | ½ TEASPOON BAKING POWDER |
| ¼ CUP MOLASSES | ½ TEASPOON BAKING SODA |
| 1 CUP WHITE SUGAR | 1 LARGE EGG |
| 1 TEASPOON GROUND GINGER | ¾ TEASPOON VANILLA EXTRACT |
| ½ TEASPOON GROUND CINNAMON | 1 CUP UNBLEACHED OR WHITE |
| ½ TEASPOON GROUND NUTMEG | PRESIFTED ALL-PURPOSE FLOUR |
| ¾ TEASPOON GROUND CLOVES | 1 ¼ CUPS UNCOOKED ROLLED OATS |
| ¼ TEASPOON SALT | ¾ CUP RAISINS |

Preheat the oven to 375°F. Grease your baking sheets.

Melt the butter and stir in the rest of the ingredients in the order listed.

Drop teaspoons of batter at least 2″ apart onto the sheets. Bake for 12 minutes. Immediately move the cookies to a wire rack with a wide spatula. Cool completely.

**MAKES 72 COOKIES**

You can buy sweetened or unsweetened toasted coconut flakes at health food stores and some fruit stands, or you can make them yourself. Spread the sweetened or unsweetened coconut flakes on a baking sheet. Bake in a 350°F. oven for about five minutes, shaking the sheet occasionally, until the flakes are light brown. These cookies have a wonderful underlying coconut taste and the rough, hearty texture of oatmeal cookies.

1¼ TEASPOONS GROUND GINGER

1 TEASPOON GROUND CLOVES

¾ TEASPOON GROUND CINNAMON

1 TEASPOON BAKING SODA

½ CUP UNSALTED BUTTER

2 TABLESPOONS MOLASSES

2 TABLESPOONS LIGHT CORN SYRUP

1 TEASPOON WHITE VINEGAR

2 LARGE EGGS

1 CUP WHITE SUGAR

1½ CUPS UNBLEACHED OR WHITE PRESIFTED ALL-PURPOSE FLOUR

1¾ CUPS TOASTED COCONUT FLAKES

Mix together the ginger, cloves, cinnamon, and baking soda and set aside. Preheat the oven to 325°F. Grease your baking sheets.

Melt the butter in a small saucepan. Remove from the heat and whisk in the molasses, corn syrup, and vinegar. Scrape into a bowl, then whisk in the spice mixture and eggs. Beat in the sugar, then the flour. Fold in the coconut.

Drop even tablespoons of the batter at least 1″ apart onto the baking sheets. Bake for 15 minutes. Immediately remove the cookies with a wide spatula to a wire rack. Wipe off the baking sheets and regrease before each batch.

**MAKES 48 COOKIES**

I adore biscotti, especially with an espresso. I also like them when I'm not feeling well, since their subtle taste and dry texture make them as comforting as toast. While Italians would be horrified at the addition of ginger, I've added only enough to give them a gentle hint of spiciness. Please try these, even though they do take time to make. Or, if you don't want to make your own, buy some, spread them with a thin layer of dark chocolate, then sprinkle the still-wet chocolate with finely chopped candied ginger and let it dry.

6 OUNCES WHOLE SHELLED
   HAZELNUTS AND/OR BLANCHED
   ALMONDS
3 LARGE EGGS
2 TABLESPOONS DARK CORN SYRUP
½ TEASPOON ALMOND EXTRACT
1½ TEASPOONS GROUND GINGER
1¼ TEASPOONS GROUND CLOVES

1 TEASPOON GROUND ALLSPICE
PINCH OF SALT
1 TEASPOON BAKING POWDER
1 CUP PLUS 2 TABLESPOONS WHITE
   SUGAR
3 CUPS UNBLEACHED OR WHITE
   PRESIFTED ALL-PURPOSE FLOUR

Heat the oven to 300°F. Place the nuts, separated if using both types, on a baking sheet. Toast in the oven for 15 minutes, shaking the sheet occasionally to prevent burning, until the nuts are light brown. Immediately place the hazelnuts in a towel and rub briskly until the brown skins peel off.

Turn the oven to 375°, and grease and flour the baking sheet.

In a large bowl lightly whisk together the eggs, corn syrup, and almond extract, then whisk in the ginger, cloves, allspice, salt, and baking powder. Beat in the sugar, then enough of the flour to make a kneadable dough. You will probably use almost all of it.

Turn the dough out onto a board lightly covered with any remaining flour. Knead the dough for about 5 minutes, until very smooth. Add the nuts and knead for another 3 or 4 minutes. Divide the dough into halves. Roll each into a 2″-wide rope.

Place the ropes onto the baking sheet and bake for 40 minutes. Remove the baking sheet from the oven and let the rolls cool on it for 10 minutes. Turn the oven down to 325°.

With a long, thin spatula remove the rolls very carefully to a cutting board. Using a serrated knife, cut each roll, on the diagonal, into 14 slices.

Rinse off the baking sheet and dry well. Place the slices on the sheet, cut side down, and bake for 15 minutes more. Immediately remove with a spatula to a wire rack and cool completely. These will keep at least a week in an airtight jar.

MAKES 28 BISCOTTI

These cookies combine two traditional British favorites—gingerbread and shortbread. Many traditional cooks prefer rice flour in shortbread rather than cornstarch, but both are authentic. If you don't want to spend the time cutting out cookies, shortbread dough can be pressed out a quarter inch thick in cake pans and scored across the top into six or eight wedges to simplify breaking apart when cooled. I use a dog-bone cookie cutter because shortbread's pale color is reminiscent of bones . . . and I have an odd sense of humor.

| | |
|---|---|
| 2 CUPS UNBLEACHED OR WHITE PRESIFTED ALL-PURPOSE FLOUR | ¼ CUP WHITE SUGAR, SUPERFINE PREFERABLE |
| ¼ CUP RICE FLOUR OR CORNSTARCH | 1 LARGE EGG |
| 1 CUP UNSALTED BUTTER, AT ROOM TEMPERATURE | 1 TABLESPOON MILK |
| | 1 TEASPOON GROUND GINGER |
| ¼ CUP BROWN SUGAR | 1 TEASPOON GROUND CINNAMON |

Preheat the oven to 325°F. Grease your baking sheets. Mix together both flours and set aside. Cream the butter, then beat in the sugars, egg, milk, ginger, and cinnamon. Beat in the flours.

Turn the dough out onto a very lightly floured board and knead a few times, just until smooth. Pat out ¼" thick. Cut into rectangles about 3" or 4" long by 1" wide, or use a cookie cutter with approximately those dimensions.

Using a spatula, place the cookies on the baking sheets. They can be as close as ½" apart. Prick each cookie with a fork until there are about 8 or 9 tiny holes. Bake for 30 minutes, just until the edges of each cookie are pale brown. Move the cookies to a wire rack with the spatula. Sprinkle with more white sugar, if desired. Cool completely.

**MAKES 36 COOKIES**

These are similar to shortbread, but are baked in cookie molds. There are molds made of thin metal with eighteen indentations in each, often in three different shapes, and there are little metal tins, each holding one cookie. They can be bought at many cookware shops or mail-ordered from the cookware stores listed on pages 179–183. While authentic sand tarts don't contain ginger, I find it adds piquancy.

½ TEASPOON GROUND GINGER

½ TEASPOON GROUND CLOVES

¼ TEASPOON GROUND CINNAMON

½ CUP UNSALTED BUTTER, AT ROOM
   TEMPERATURE

6 TABLESPOONS CONFECTIONERS'
   SUGAR

2 TABLESPOONS HONEY

1 LARGE EGG YOLK

1 CUP UNBLEACHED OR WHITE
   PRESIFTED ALL-PURPOSE FLOUR

Preheat the oven to 375°F. Butter the cookie molds.

Mix together the ginger, cloves, and cinnamon and set aside. Beat the butter, sugar, honey, and egg yolk until smooth. Beat in the spices, then the flour.

Drop about 2 teaspoons of batter into each indentation. When all the indentations are filled, flatten the batter in each with dampened fingers. Bake for 7 to 8 minutes, until lightly browned around the edges.

Cool the molds on a wire rack. When the cookies are room temperature, they can be easily turned out.

**MAKES 36 SAND TARTS**

These are almost more like candy than cookies. They are terrific eaten on their own, or they can be shaped while hot to make delicious domes for draping over scoops of banana, praline, vanilla, or even chocolate ice cream. Drizzle hot fudge over the ice cream and its cage. If you have any extra cookies, break them into tiny pieces and fold into vanilla ice cream along with some Caramel Sauce (see recipe, page 57) to create praline ice cream.

½ CUP UNSALTED BUTTER

½ CUP BROWN SUGAR

¼ CUP MOLASSES

½ TEASPOON GROUND GINGER

½ TEASPOON GROUND CLOVES

¼ TEASPOON GROUND CINNAMON

1 TABLESPOON BRANDY OR COGNAC

¾ CUP UNBLEACHED OR WHITE PRESIFTED ALL-PURPOSE FLOUR

Preheat the oven to 350°F. Cut aluminum foil into 16 squares, large enough to fit just 4 on your baking sheets. Grease the foil squares and set them aside.

In a large saucepan heat the butter, sugar, and molasses over very low heat, stirring often, until smooth. While the butter mixture is heating, mix together the ginger, cloves, and cinnamon. When the butter mixture is smooth, stir in the spices and brandy or cognac, then the flour. Remove the pan from the heat. Beat well to get rid of any lumps.

Place 4 foil squares on each of 2 baking sheets. Drop the mixture by teaspoons into the center of the squares. Bake for 8 minutes, then carefully slide the foil squares off the baking sheets onto your workspace. Begin baking 8 more cookies.

Cool the cookies on the foil until they're no longer liquid, 5 to 10 minutes. When solid enough to move, transfer them with a spatula from the foil to a paper towel–covered wire rack. Or drape the cookies, foil side up, over upside-down small bowls or cups to create domes or bowls. Peel off the foil as soon as possible. Remove the cookies from the bowls when they are completely solid.

**MAKES 42 COOKIES**

These are adapted from a Scandinavian cookie which, like many Scandinavian cookies, has the buttery taste of shortbread. I find the ginger cuts the richness in an agreeable way. You can form these into any shape you choose, but the ones below are traditional.

¾ TEASPOON GROUND GINGER

¾ TEASPOON GROUND CLOVES

½ TEASPOON GROUND CARDAMOM

½ TEASPOON GROUND CINNAMON

PINCH OF SALT

½ CUP UNSALTED BUTTER

⅔ CUP BROWN SUGAR

½ TEASPOON VANILLA EXTRACT

⅔ CUP BUTTERMILK

2 CUPS UNBLEACHED OR WHITE PRESIFTED ALL-PURPOSE FLOUR

1—1¼ CUPS WHITE SUGAR

Mix together the ginger, cloves, cardamom, cinnamon, and salt and set aside. Melt the butter in a small saucepan. Remove from the heat and stir in the brown sugar until dissolved. Scrape into a bowl. Stir the spice mixture into the bowl. Beat in the vanilla and buttermilk, then the flour. Form the dough into a ball. Chill, well wrapped in plastic, for at least 2 hours and preferably overnight.

Preheat the oven to 350°F. Grease 2 baking sheets. Handling the dough as little as possible, roll it into five ¼"-thick ropes on a surface dusted with some of the white sugar. Keep adding sugar as necessary. Refrigerate all the ropes but one. Cut the rope into 8 lengths. Shape each piece into a pretzel or figure eight.

Place the cookies as soon as they're made at least 1" apart on the baking sheets. Form the rest of the cookies. Bake for 20 minutes, until the sugary edges are browned. Don't worry if the cookies seem to spread and burn; it's only the sugar and you can cut that part off. Remove the cookies from the oven and let them sit on the baking sheet for a minute before moving them to a wire rack to cool. As you remove them from the sheet, the burnt edges will crack off (or break them off yourself).

MAKES 40 COOKIES

Fried cookies are popular celebration fare throughout the world. German strübli, krapfen, and flädli; Norwegian fattigmand; Danish ægte Danske klejner; and what we in America call Italian bow ties are just a few examples. Unlike most gingerbread cookies, which are delicious the next day when they've mellowed, these must be eaten within a few hours after they're made or they become leaden. Form the dough into any fairly flat shape; just be sure the cookies are not too thick at any point or the dough in the center will remain uncooked.

| | |
|---|---|
| ½ TEASPOON GROUND GINGER | 1 CUP UNBLEACHED OR WHITE |
| ½ TEASPOON GROUND CLOVES | PRESIFTED ALL-PURPOSE FLOUR |
| ¼ TEASPOON GROUND CARDAMOM | LARD OR TASTELESS VEGETABLE OIL |
| 1 LARGE EGG PLUS 1 LARGE YOLK | 3 TABLESPOONS CONFECTIONERS' |
| 1 TABLESPOON HEAVY CREAM | SUGAR |
| 3 TABLESPOONS BROWN SUGAR | |

Mix together the ginger, cloves, and cardamom and set aside. Beat the egg, yolk, and cream until smooth. Beat in the sugar and the spice mixture. Gently stir in the flour just until combined.

On a lightly floured board roll the dough out $\frac{1}{16}''$ thick. Cut into diamonds about 4″ long by 2½″ wide. Cut a 2″ slit in the center of each along the 4″ length. Pull the point at the top of the 4″ length through the slit. Slightly pinch it to the rest of the cookie to secure it. Brush off any excess flour.

Pour the lard or oil into a skillet to a depth of 1″. Heat until very hot but not smoking. Deep-fry the cookies, 3 or 4 at a time, until golden brown. Drain well on paper towels, then cool on a rack. If the cookies brown too quickly, turn down the heat slightly and for just the next batch cook 5 or 6 cookies at once. Sprinkle the cooled cookies with the confectioners' sugar.

**MAKES 18 COOKIES**

Once found only in Jewish bakeries, these are now sold throughout America. The cream cheese pastry is very rich, but not greasy; it also makes a good piecrust. Don't overwork the dough, however, or it will become very tough. You can use any kind of dried fruit—apricots, prunes, and pears are especially good—instead of raisins, but the caramelized sugar in slightly burnt raisins is wonderful.

| | |
|---|---|
| 1 CUP PLUS 6 TABLESPOONS UNSALTED BUTTER | ¼ TEASPOON GROUND CLOVES |
| ½ POUND CREAM CHEESE | ¼ TEASPOON SALT |
| 2 LARGE EGGS | 3 CUPS UNBLEACHED OR WHITE PRESIFTED ALL-PURPOSE FLOUR |
| ¼ CUP MOLASSES | 1 ⅓ CUPS RAISINS |
| 1 ¼ TEASPOONS GROUND GINGER | 1 ⅓ CUPS FINELY CHOPPED WALNUTS |
| 1 ¼ TEASPOONS GROUND CINNAMON | 1 ⅓ CUPS BROWN SUGAR |
| ½ TEASPOON GROUND NUTMEG | |

Beat or process 1 cup butter and the cream cheese together until smooth. Lightly whisk together the eggs, molasses, ginger, cinnamon, nutmeg, cloves, and salt, then beat well into the cream cheese mixture. Beat in the flour just until completely mixed.

Form the dough into 8 balls, wrap in plastic, and refrigerate for 30 minutes to 2 days.

When ready to make the cookies, mix together the raisins, nuts, and brown sugar in a bowl. Remove one ball of dough from the refrigerator. On a lightly floured board pat the dough out into a small circle, then quickly roll it into a 6″ circle. Cut it into 6 wedges, but don't move them.

Melt the 6 tablespoons butter. Brush the dough circle with the butter, then scatter 2 small handfuls of the nut mixture on it. Lightly press the nuts and raisins into the dough without breaking through. Starting with the outside edges of the circle, roll the wedges up, croissant style, to enclose the nuts and raisins. If any of the nuts and raisins fall out, push them back into place. Move the rolled cookies to a greased baking sheet, point side down. Curve the cookies slightly to make crescents.

Make the rest of the cookies the same way. When you've made half the cookies, begin preheating the oven to 350°F. When all the cookies are on the baking sheets, brush them with any remaining melted butter. Bake for 25 minutes, until browned all over. Cool on wire racks.

**MAKES 48 RUGELACH**

These cookies have the crisp and chewy texture found in lacy cookies like Florentines. You can make sandwiches as I've done, spread each individual cookie with chocolate, or eat them plain. If you prefer, use semisweet or milk chocolate. The cookies can be stored, before the chocolate is added, for up to a week in an airtight container. They do become harder and less chewy over time, so judge accordingly. The sandwiches can be stored for two or three days.

| | |
|---|---|
| ½ TEASPOON GROUND GINGER | 1 CUP WHITE SUGAR |
| ½ TEASPOON GROUND CINNAMON | ½ CUP BROWN SUGAR |
| ¼ TEASPOON GROUND CARDAMOM | 3 LARGE EGGS |
| ⅛ TEASPOON GROUND CLOVES | 1 ¼ CUPS UNBLEACHED OR WHITE |
| ⅛ TEASPOON GROUND NUTMEG | PRESIFTED ALL-PURPOSE FLOUR |
| ¾ CUP UNSALTED BUTTER | 6 OUNCES BITTERSWEET CHOCOLATE |
| ½ CUP MOLASSES | |

Preheat the oven to 350°F. Grease and flour rimmed baking sheets. Mix together the ginger, cinnamon, cardamom, cloves, and nutmeg and set aside.

Melt the butter in a small saucepan, then remove from the heat. Stir in the molasses and both sugars, then the spice mixture. Beat in the eggs well, then the flour, until completely incorporated.

Drop balls of batter, about 2 teaspoons each, onto the baking sheets. Leave 3″ between the cookies and the sides of the sheet. Prod the cookies with a damp finger into as perfect a circle as possible. Bake for 12 to

15 minutes, until the edges are just slightly browner than the rest of the cookie. If the cookies begin to spread and run into each other, prod them back into shape with a spatula after the first 3 minutes. Using a spatula, remove the still-soft baked cookies to a rack to cool. Bake the rest of the cookies the same way.

When all the cookies have cooled, melt the chocolate. While the chocolate is melting, match up pairs of cookies with similar shapes. Spread the flat side of one of each cookie pair with melted chocolate, then press the flat side of the second cookie onto the chocolate. Cool on a rack until the chocolate has solidified.

**MAKES 30 SANDWICHES OR 60 INDIVIDUAL COOKIES**

This recipe was inspired by Judith Olney's perfect chocolate madeleines in *The Joy of Chocolate*. Since chocolate and ginger are an excellent combination, this recipe was inevitable. Like all madeleines, these taste more like little pound cakes than cookies. While it always seems ridiculous to me to clutter up the kitchen with another specialized pan, I find a madeleine mold very useful. I make chocolate candy shells or shape ice cream in it, or bake miniature cheesecakes, corn sticks, pastry shells for hors d'oeuvres, and other flavored madeleines with nuts, lemon, vanilla, or mint.

2½ TEASPOONS GROUND GINGER

2 TEASPOONS GROUND CINNAMON

1 TEASPOON GROUND NUTMEG

¾ TEASPOON GROUND CLOVES

¾ TEASPOON GROUND CARDAMOM

2 TABLESPOONS UNSWEETENED COCOA POWDER, SIEVED TO RID OF LUMPS

PINCH OF SALT

¾ CUP UNSALTED BUTTER

3½ OUNCES SEMISWEET CHOCOLATE

¼ CUP BROWN SUGAR

½ CUP WHITE SUGAR

5 LARGE EGGS, LIGHTLY BEATEN

1½ CUPS UNBLEACHED OR WHITE PRESIFTED ALL-PURPOSE FLOUR

Mix together the ginger, cinnamon, nutmeg, cloves, cardamom, cocoa, and salt and set aside. Preheat the oven to 350°F. Grease the molds.

Melt the butter and chocolate together in a medium-size saucepan. Remove from the heat and stir in the sugars, then the spice mixture. Beat in the eggs thoroughly. Fold in 1 cup of the flour, then the remaining ½ cup.

Place 1 heaping tablespoon of the mixture into each greased madeleine mold indentation. When the molds are full, bang them on the counter once or twice to even out the filling. If necessary, gently flatten the filling with slightly damp fingers.

Bake the cookies for 10 to 12 minutes, until a skewer in the center of one comes out clean. Turn out onto a wire rack to cool.

**MAKES 40 MADELEINES**

These cookies are a natural since, according to Betty Fussell in *I Hear America Cooking*, the original "tollhouse cookies" were adapted from a recipe in a 1796 cookbook included under the heading of "Gingerbread Cakes or Butter and Sugar Gingerbread." If the batter is not completely cooled or you beat too hard when you add the chocolate, the chips will melt. Don't worry. Immediately stop beating the batter and begin dropping the cookies onto the baking sheet. You now have lovely chocolate swirl cookies. Be sure you use excellent chocolate in these. Otherwise, why bother?

1 ¼ TEASPOONS GROUND GINGER

¾ TEASPOON GROUND CINNAMON

½ TEASPOON GROUND NUTMEG

1 TEASPOON GROUND CLOVES

PINCH OF SALT

1 CUP UNSALTED BUTTER

1 CUP BROWN SUGAR

2 TABLESPOONS MOLASSES

1 LARGE EGG

2 CUPS UNBLEACHED OR WHITE PRESIFTED ALL-PURPOSE FLOUR

6–7 OUNCES SEMISWEET OR BITTERSWEET CHOCOLATE CHIPS OR CHUNKS

Preheat the oven to 350°F. Grease and flour your baking sheets. Mix together the ginger, cinnamon, nutmeg, cloves, and salt and set aside.

Melt the butter in a small saucepan. Remove the saucepan from the heat and beat in the sugar and molasses. Scrape the butter mixture into a bowl. Beat in the spice mixture, then the egg, then the flour. Let cool to room temperature. Gently fold the chocolate into the cooled mixture.

Drop heaping teaspoons of batter at least 2″ apart onto the baking sheets. Bake for 10 minutes. As soon as the cookies are solid enough to move, move them with a spatula to a wire rack.

**MAKES 52 COOKIES**

# PEANUT BUTTER COOKIES
## WITH BUTTERSCOTCH CHIPS

Peanut butter cookies are either very good or very bad. My nephew Brian Onufrychuk helped me create these, and no one knows peanut butter cookies better than a six-year-old. If you want nuts in your cookies, add pecans or walnuts. I never use chunky peanut butter, though, since the peanut taste then becomes overwhelming and the pieces get stuck in your teeth.

¾ TEASPOON GROUND GINGER

¾ TEASPOON GROUND CINNAMON

½ TEASPOON GROUND CLOVES

½ TEASPOON GROUND NUTMEG

PINCH OF SALT

1 TEASPOON BAKING POWDER

¼ TEASPOON BAKING SODA

½ CUP UNSALTED BUTTER, AT ROOM TEMPERATURE

½ CUP SMOOTH PEANUT BUTTER

1 LARGE EGG

½ TEASPOON VANILLA EXTRACT

2 TABLESPOONS DARK CORN SYRUP

1 CUP BROWN SUGAR

1½ CUPS UNBLEACHED OR WHITE PRESIFTED ALL-PURPOSE FLOUR

¾ CUP BUTTERSCOTCH CHIPS

Preheat the oven to 375°F. Grease your baking sheets. Mix together the ginger, cinnamon, cloves, nutmeg, salt, baking powder, and baking soda and set aside.

Beat the butter and peanut butter together until smooth. Beat in, in the following order, the egg, vanilla, corn syrup, spice mixture, sugar, and flour. Gently fold in the butterscotch chips.

Roll the mixture into 1″-diameter balls, then flatten until about 1½″ across. Place the cookies at least 1″ apart on the baking sheets. Bake for 13 to 15 minutes, until lightly browned around the edges or all over, depending on your preference. Move the cookies to a wire rack with a wide spatula and cool completely.

**MAKES 42 COOKIES**

Adapted from the classic French cookie, these can easily be molded into "bowls" or other decorative shapes. I like them best as "taco shells" (see Berry "Tacos," page 83) or plain. Elegant, adult cookies, these are perfect alongside ice cream or a dessert soufflé.

| | |
|---|---|
| 3 LARGE EGG WHITES | ½ TEASPOON GROUND NUTMEG |
| ½ CUP WHITE SUGAR | 6 TABLESPOONS UNSALTED BUTTER, |
| 1 TABLESPOON HONEY | MELTED AND COOLED |
| 2 TABLESPOONS MOLASSES | ½ CUP UNBLEACHED OR WHITE |
| ½ TEASPOON VANILLA EXTRACT | PRESIFTED ALL-PURPOSE FLOUR |
| 1 TEASPOON GROUND GINGER | ½ CUP FINELY CHOPPED BLANCHED |
| 1 TEASPOON GROUND CINNAMON | ALMONDS |

Preheat the oven to 350°F. Grease the baking sheets. Whisk together the egg whites, sugar, honey, molasses, and vanilla. Whisk in the ginger, cinnamon, and nutmeg, then the butter. Then stir or whisk in the flour and nuts just till mixed.

Drop the mixture by level tablespoons at least 3″ apart onto a baking sheet. Bake the sheets one at a time (5 or 6 cookies per sheet) or at 5 minute intervals. Bake for 8 to 10 minutes, until the cookies brown around the edges. Quickly remove the cookies from the sheet with a spatula and drape over a rolling pin or thick wooden dowel. Continue to make the rest of the cookies, greasing each sheet well before each batch. As soon as the draped cookies are stiff, which should only take about 5 minutes, remove them to a wire rack to cool completely.

**MAKES 25 COOKIES**

These are closer to the flat English macaroons than the thicker American kind. Try to find edible rice paper at a bakery supply store, since it's so easy to use, though cooking parchment works almost as well. Macaroons are delicious in trifle, or they can be crushed and used instead of gingersnap or graham cracker crumbs in many desserts, such as Baked Apples (see recipe, page 85). The addition of the sugar to the almonds as they're ground prevents them from becoming too pasty. If you can find boxed ground almonds, substitute them for the whole ones.

| | |
|---|---|
| 5 OUNCES BLANCHED ALMONDS (ABOUT 1 ¼ CUPS) | ½ TEASPOON GROUND GINGER |
| 1 ¼ CUPS WHITE SUGAR | ½ TEASPOON GROUND CINNAMON |
| ½ TEASPOON ALMOND EXTRACT | ½ TEASPOON GROUND NUTMEG |
| | 2 EGG WHITES |

Grind the almonds in a nut grinder or food processor with 2 tablespoons of the sugar until powdery. Turn the nuts out into a bowl if you used the grinder or continue in the processor. Beat or process in the remaining ingredients until well mixed.

Preheat the oven to 325°F. Cover your baking sheets with rice paper or greased and floured parchment. Roll the mixture into 1″-diameter balls. Place the balls at least 2″ apart on the baking sheet. Bake for 20 minutes. Set up uncooked balls on baking sheet–size rice paper or parchment while the first batch is cooking.

If you're using parchment, immediately remove the macaroons with a spatula as soon as they come out of the oven; cool on a wire rack. If you're using rice paper, move the whole sheet of paper to the rack. Cut or tear around the paper and cookies when they're cool, since they're eaten paper and all.

**MAKES 26 COOKIES**

# FORTUNE COOKIES

These are crisper than the traditional fortune cookie—and also a lot tastier. They're great party cookies. Write fortunes tailored to your guests or use quotes from poetry, politicians, philosophers, or films. My favorite comes from the movie *The Adventures of Buckaroo Banzai*: "No matter where you go, there you are." It always seems applicable.

3 LARGE EGG WHITES

½ CUP WHITE SUGAR

1 TABLESPOON HONEY

¼ TEASPOON SALT

1 TEASPOON GROUND GINGER

1 TEASPOON GROUND CINNAMON

½ TEASPOON GROUND NUTMEG

6 TABLESPOONS UNSALTED BUTTER, MELTED AND COOLED

½ CUP UNBLEACHED OR WHITE PRESIFTED ALL-PURPOSE FLOUR

Type out the fortunes on a sheet of paper, then cut into thin strips 4½″ to 5″ long. Preheat the oven to 325°F. Grease the baking sheets.

Whisk together the egg whites, sugar, and honey. Whisk in the salt, ginger, cinnamon, and nutmeg, then the butter. Beat or whisk in the flour just until mixed.

Be very careful to use no more than a level tablespoon for each cookie, or they will be too large. Drop the cookies at least 3″ apart onto the baking sheet. Using the back of a spoon or a butter knife, spread the cookies out to form even 3″-diameter circles. Bake the sheets one at a time (5 or 6 cookies per sheet) or at 5 minute intervals. Bake for 10 minutes, until the cookies are lightly browned around the edges.

Remove the sheet from the oven. Let the cookies cool on the sheet for about 10 seconds, until you can slip a spatula under one without tearing it apart. You now need to work very quickly. Remove one cookie and place it top side down on your counter. Lay a fortune across the center, sticking out on one side. Fold the cookie over the fortune, then quickly push the ends of the flat side toward each other to form the traditional fortune cookie shape. Form the rest of the baked cookies, then place them on a rack to cool. Regrease the baking sheet well before each batch.

**MAKES 40 COOKIES**

# THUMBPRINT COOKIES

These are popular throughout Europe, often with interesting names such as hussar balls or pits of love. The version found in American bakeries is almost invariably unspiced. While I prefer the varieties of preserves listed below, you may use whichever kind you like.

3 LARGE EGGS

1 TEASPOON VANILLA EXTRACT

1 ½ TEASPOONS GROUND GINGER

1 ¼ TEASPOONS GROUND CINNAMON

¾ TEASPOON GROUND CLOVES

¼ TEASPOON GROUND CARDAMOM

DASH OF SALT

2 ¼ CUPS FINELY CHOPPED PECANS
   OR WALNUTS

1 CUP UNSALTED BUTTER, AT ROOM
   TEMPERATURE

½ CUP BROWN SUGAR

2 CUPS UNBLEACHED OR WHITE
   PRESIFTED ALL-PURPOSE FLOUR

½ CUP PLUS 2 TABLESPOONS
   RASPBERRY, STRAWBERRY, OR
   APRICOT JAM OR PRESERVES

Preheat the oven to 375°F. Grease your baking sheets.

Separate 2 of the eggs. Lightly whisk together the whole egg, 2 yolks, vanilla, ginger, cinnamon, cloves, cardamom, and salt. Place the 2 egg whites in one small bowl, the nuts in another. Beat the butter and sugar until smooth, then beat in the egg and spice mixture. Beat in the flour, one-third at a time.

Roll the dough into 1″ diameter balls. Dip each cookie into the egg whites, then roll in the nuts. Place about 1″ apart on the baking sheets.

Make an indentation in the center of each cookie with your thumb or a thimble, pressing as deeply as possible without going through the bottom. The indentation must be centered and even or the filling will run out. Spoon ½ teaspoon jam or preserves into each cookie. The filling should be slightly heaping. Bake for 15 minutes. The cookies will still be pale, but they're cooked through.

Immediately remove the cookies with a spatula to a rack. If any of the filling runs out during baking, top off the cookie with a little more as it comes out of the oven. Cool to room temperature.

**MAKES 60 COOKIES**

British gingerbreads are often baked in a pan, then cut into rectangles like this. You can substitute molasses for all or part of the honey in this recipe if you want darker cookies, but I prefer the lighter version. Butterscotch chips are also good in these chewy bars.

2 TEASPOONS BAKING POWDER

½ TEASPOON SALT

1½ TEASPOONS GROUND GINGER

1½ TEASPOONS GROUND CINNAMON

½ TEASPOON GROUND NUTMEG

½ TEASPOON GROUND CLOVES

½ CUP UNSALTED BUTTER

1½ CUPS BROWN SUGAR

¼ CUP MOLASSES

¼ CUP HONEY

3 LARGE EGGS

1 TEASPOON VANILLA EXTRACT

2 CUPS UNBLEACHED OR WHITE PRESIFTED ALL-PURPOSE FLOUR

¾ CUP ROUGHLY CHOPPED WALNUTS OR PECANS

2 CUPS SEMISWEET CHOCOLATE CHUNKS

Preheat the oven to 350°F. Grease a 10"-x-15"-x-1" jelly-roll pan or 10"-x-14" roasting pan.

Mix together the baking powder, salt, ginger, cinnamon, nutmeg, and cloves and set aside.

Melt the butter in a small saucepan. Remove from the heat and immediately stir in the sugar, molasses, and honey. Scrape out into a bowl. Beat the spice mixture, eggs, and vanilla into the butter mixture. Fold in the flour, then the nuts, then the chocolate. Don't mix too much after the chocolate is added, so the chunks will remain fairly large.

Pour the batter into the pan and bake for about 35 minutes, until a skewer inserted into the center of the pan comes out clean. (Don't confuse the melted chocolate on the skewer with raw batter, however.) Remove the pan from the oven and place on a rack to cool. When cool, cut into fourths lengthwise, then cut each strip into sixths.

**MAKES 24 BARS**

The chocolate in this recipe mellows out the fresh ginger, so the taste of these isn't jarring to unsuspecting tasters. While I usually prefer unfrosted brownies, any kind of caramel icing is delicious on these. Begin making the frosting as soon as you take the brownies out of the oven, then spread it on as soon as it's done. For an incomparable sundae, top an unfrosted brownie with sliced bananas, add a scoop of banana ice cream, spoon over caramel, butterscotch, brandy, or rum sauce, and add a dollop of unsweetened whipped cream.

2 TEASPOONS GROUND NUTMEG

2 TEASPOONS GROUND GINGER

1 TEASPOON GROUND CLOVES

2½ TEASPOONS GROUND CINNAMON

1 TEASPOON BAKING POWDER

1 CUP UNSALTED BUTTER

8 OUNCES UNSWEETENED
CHOCOLATE

1 CUP BROWN SUGAR

1½ CUPS WHITE SUGAR

¼ CUP HONEY

5 LARGE EGGS

1 TABLESPOON FINELY GRATED
FRESH GINGER

1½ CUPS UNBLEACHED OR WHITE
PRESIFTED ALL-PURPOSE FLOUR

½ CUP ROUGHLY CHOPPED WALNUTS
(OPTIONAL)

Preheat the oven to 350°F. Grease an 8″-x-14″-x-2″ baking pan. Mix together the nutmeg, ground ginger, cloves, cinnamon, and baking powder and set aside.

Melt the butter and chocolate together in a small saucepan. Remove the pan from the heat and stir in both sugars and the honey. Scrape the chocolate mixture into a bowl and stir in the spice mixture. Beat in the eggs and fresh ginger, then the flour. Fold in the nuts, if used.

Pour the batter into the baking pan. Bake for about 45 minutes, until a skewer inserted into the brownies comes out clean. Place the pan on a wire rack. When cool, cut lengthwise into fourths, then cut each strip into fourths.

**MAKES 16 BROWNIES**

T he best thing about gingerbread cake, aside from the fact that it tastes wonderful, is that it's really difficult to make a bad one. It was a popular cake during rationing days since cooks could replace fresh milk with evaporated or sour milk, sour cream, or buttermilk. Any fat works—animal, dairy, or vegetable. You can use one egg or several. If you don't have enough of one flour or sweetener, combine two or even three kinds. It's even almost impossible to overmix the batter, since it can take a lot of beating.

While gingerbread cakes around the world all start with the same basic recipe, there are some unique variations. Pureed or chopped fruits or vegetables added to the batter for both moisture and flavor often identify the country of origin. For example, in the Caribbean they use bananas, carrots, soursop, potatoes, sweet potatoes, pumpkin, and breadfruit. Americans are also fond of banana gingerbread, while the British bake rhubarb in theirs. The Swiss are partial to carrot, Czechs enjoy plum, and Liberians like plantains. The frugal Swedes bake a cake after Christmas flavored with the fruit served in the alcoholic holiday punch. Gingerbread with apples or applesauce in it or on top is popular everywhere. One thing these cakes have in common is that they're rarely served plain, as the dense cake is the perfect foil for something creamy or tart or both. Toppings of whipped cream, fruit, lemon sauce or icing, and ice cream are all international favorites.

Unless I've specified otherwise in the recipe, most of the gingerbread cakes below are original rather than traditional. Gingerbreads are underutilized as layer cakes in America, so I've provided quite a few versions in this chapter. In eastern Europe, cakes are often split horizontally, the inside spread with jam, then the top replaced. Gingerbread jelly rolls—whether filled with prune butter in eastern Europe or gingered whipped cream in New York—are elegant enough for any formal dinner.

There are several important tips to remember when baking cakes. Always grease or grease and flour (whichever the recipe demands) the pans thoroughly, or the cake will stick. Make sure the batter in a paperlined pan is as deep in the corners as it is in the center, or the corners will burn. Whipped egg whites and cream are added to a cake to increase the volume; gently fold rather than beat them in, or they will deflate. When flour is added to a cake batter with more than one egg, it should be mixed as little as possible, or the cake will be rubbery. It's easy to tell when a cake is done; a skewer or toothpick inserted into the center and almost to the bottom can be removed without any batter sticking to it.

You can substitute a cake pan of a different shape if it has approximately the same volume as the one specified in the recipe. Generally, deep cakes take longer to bake than thin ones, regardless of the volume. For example, a recipe that calls for a nine-inch round cake pan can be baked in an eight-inch square one. If you have only a nine- inch square pan, the thinner cake will cook more quickly. If you can find them, adjustable pans are wonderful. There are loaf pans, often used for pâtés, which stretch out to almost twice the normal length, and rectangular cake pans which have blocks you can place in them to form a smaller or unusually shaped cake. If you have room in your kitchen for another piece of equipment, a checkerboard cake kit is something to consider, since children marvel at cakes created with it. As a rule, I prefer the shiny silver pans, since the black nonstick variety seem to brown the bottom and sides of the cake more. If you prefer nonstick, then feel free to use them in any of the recipes below.

Very dense cakes, such as the basic gingerbread cake, can be stored for at least a week tightly wrapped in foil. They are usually best the second through the fifth day, since they've had time to mellow but not lose their taste. If you want to get a head start on layer cakes, bake the layers but don't frost them. Wrap them tightly in foil and store at room temperature for a day or so or in the freezer for up to three months. Butter-based frostings can be refrigerated in an airtight container for up to a week, but must be brought to room temperature and beaten until smooth before using. Frost your cake as close to serving time as possible.

Frosted cakes can be refrigerated if you have a butter-based frosting, but the cake will become slightly soggy within a day. Don't freeze frosted cakes, since the texture of the frosting deteriorates. If you absolutely must make a cake ahead and won't have time to frost it later, try a torte or cheesecake. Many tortes are so rich they don't require frosting, while cheesecakes can be frozen for several months with almost no discernible change in taste or texture.

When creating a gingerbread cake, I begin with about 1¾ teaspoons of spice for each cup of flour (or any other major dry ingredient, such as oats). The spice mixture usually includes equal amounts of ginger and cinnamon or cloves, then smaller amounts of allspice, nutmeg, and/or cardamom. If your cake includes two kinds of batter, the gingerbread batter should be slightly spicier than usual to compensate for the lack of spicing in the other batter.

Though originally considered a bread, this is now invariably served as cake. It is still, however, surprisingly good toasted and spread with butter for breakfast. Topped with plain or whipped cream, crème fraîche, ice cream, lemon curd, lemon sauce, applesauce, butterscotch sauce, or hard sauce, it's an appropriate dessert for everything from a traditional New England shore dinner to Tex-Mex tacos.

Try experimenting with the ingredients. Substitute cardamom or allspice for some of the other spices. Replace part of the flour with whole wheat or rye. Add grated lemon or orange rind. If you're not crazy about molasses, honey is also good. Just keep tasting the batter as you go and you'll produce a perfect cake.

| | |
|---|---|
| 3 LARGE EGGS | ½ CUP UNSALTED BUTTER |
| 1 ½ TEASPOONS GROUND GINGER | ½ CUP MOLASSES |
| 1 ½ TEASPOONS GROUND CINNAMON | ½ CUP BROWN SUGAR |
| ¼ TEASPOON GROUND NUTMEG | ¼ CUP WATER |
| ¼ TEASPOON GROUND CLOVES | 2 CUPS UNBLEACHED OR WHITE |
| 1 TEASPOON BAKING SODA | PRESIFTED ALL-PURPOSE FLOUR |
| ½ TEASPOON SALT | |

Preheat the oven to 350°F. Grease a 7″ square pan. Whisk together the eggs, ginger, cinnamon, nutmeg, cloves, baking soda, and salt and set aside.

Melt the butter in a small saucepan. Remove from the heat and beat in the molasses and sugar. Stir in the water, then the egg and spice mixture, then the flour.

Pour the batter into the pan. Bake for 50 minutes, until a skewer inserted into the center comes out clean. Serve warm or at room temperature.

**MAKES 6 SERVINGS**

The apricot glaze and crystallized ginger transform this from a traditional midwestern family dessert to a more formal dessert. The apples dissolve into the cake, leaving it very moist and dense. When I mince the crystallized ginger, I usually discard any sugar that falls off onto the cutting board since the cake is already sweet enough. If you like crystallized ginger, use ½ cup; if you love it, use ¾ cup.

2 TEASPOONS GROUND GINGER

2¼ TEASPOONS GROUND CINNAMON

½ TEASPOON GROUND NUTMEG

¼ TEASPOON GROUND CLOVES

1 TEASPOON BAKING SODA

¾ TEASPOON SALT

¾ CUP UNSALTED BUTTER

½ CUP MOLASSES

1 CUP BROWN SUGAR

½–¾ CUP FINELY CHOPPED

CRYSTALLIZED GINGER

1½ CUPS PEELED, CORED, FINELY CHOPPED OR GRATED TART APPLES (APPROXIMATELY 2 ½-POUND APPLES)

3 LARGE EGGS

3 CUPS UNBLEACHED OR WHITE PRESIFTED ALL-PURPOSE FLOUR

½ CUP APRICOT PRESERVES

Preheat the oven to 350°F. Grease a 9½″ round springform pan. Mix together the ground ginger, cinnamon, nutmeg, cloves, baking soda, and salt and set aside.

Melt the butter in a small saucepan. Remove from the heat and stir in the molasses and sugar. Scrape out into a large bowl. Stir the spice mixture and the crystallized ginger into the bowl. Beat in the apples, then add the eggs, one at a time. Stir in the flour, one-third at a time, just until each batch is completely incorporated. The batter will be very stiff, but the apples release a lot of moisture while they're cooking.

Pour the batter into the springform pan. Bake for about 80 to 90 minutes, until a skewer inserted into the middle comes out clean. Place the pan on a rack. When the pan is cool enough to handle, remove it and replace the cake on the rack.

When the cake is almost room temperature, heat the apricot preserves over medium-high heat in a small saucepan. If the preserves contain large pieces of fruit, mash them with a wooden spoon as they heat. Heat to 210°, or until they lightly coat a spoon. They will boil gently while heating, so stir often to prevent burning.

Pour or spoon two-thirds of the preserves onto the top of the cake. There will be a rim around the top of the cake that will catch the glaze and prevent it from dripping down the sides. Quickly smooth the hot glaze evenly over the top. Then, using a small knife or cake-decorating spatula, spread the remaining glaze around the sides of the cake. Cool to room temperature.

If you prefer, you can top the cake slices with whipped cream and berries or sliced poached peaches rather than the caramel sauce. You can also try other kinds of ice cream, but keep in mind that chocolate and other stronger flavors overwhelm the delicate taste of this cake. This cake is best made the day before you plan to serve it, since the ginger taste becomes stronger over time.

| | |
|---|---|
| 6 LARGE EGGS, SEPARATED | 2 TABLESPOONS UNSALTED BUTTER, |
| 1 ¼ TEASPOONS GROUND GINGER | AT ROOM TEMPERATURE |
| 1 ¼ TEASPOONS GROUND CINNAMON | ½ CUP BROWN SUGAR |
| ¼ TEASPOON GROUND CLOVES | 1 CUP UNBLEACHED OR WHITE |
| ½ TEASPOON BAKING POWDER | PRESIFTED ALL-PURPOSE FLOUR |
| 2 TABLESPOONS MOLASSES | 1 ½ QUARTS VANILLA, PRALINE, OR |
| ¼ CUP STRONG COFFEE | PEACH ICE CREAM |

Preheat the oven to 350°F. Butter the four corners and a couple of spots in the middle of two 10″-x-15″ jelly-roll pans. Press a 17″ length of waxed paper onto each pan, leaving 1″ overhanging each of the short ends. Press the paper into the corners, then butter the paper well.

Lightly mix together the egg yolks, ginger, cinnamon, cloves, baking powder, molasses, and coffee. Place the butter in a bowl and whisk the spice mixture into it. When it's thoroughly mixed, whisk in the sugar until the mixture is smooth. Then, slowly, whisk or fold in the flour just until thoroughly moistened. Don't overmix.

Beat the egg whites until they hold stiff peaks. Stir one-quarter of the whites into the batter to lighten it. Fold in the remaining whites, about a third at a time. Spoon half the batter into each of the jelly-roll pans.

Smooth the top, making sure you have an even layer. Bake for 10 minutes, until a skewer stuck into the center of the cake comes out clean.

While the cake is baking, spread 2 smooth, slightly damp cloth kitchen towels out on your counter. Remove the baked layers from the oven, pick up the overhanging ends of the waxed paper, and flip each onto a towel, paper side up. Carefully peel off the paper and cover each layer with another slightly dampened towel. If a little of the cake is crisp, the damp towels will soften it. Let the layers cool thoroughly. Ten minutes before you're ready to complete the roll, remove the ice cream from the freezer to let it soften.

Remove the top towel and spread half the ice cream on one cake layer. Roll it up like a jelly roll, beginning at one short end. Stop when you've got about 1″ left to roll. Place the second layer so that one short end meets the still-to-be-rolled short end of the first layer. Quickly spread the remaining ice cream on the second layer and continue to roll the cake, including the second layer. Carefully place the cake on a large sheet of foil. Push any ice cream coming out of the ends back in, tightly wrap the cake in the foil, and freeze it for 1 to 24 hours.

Remove the roll from the freezer 15 minutes before you're ready to serve it. Slice off the ragged ends, then cut the cake into 12 slices. Serve with the Caramel Sauce (recipe follows) on the side.

**MAKES 12 SERVINGS**

# CARAMEL SAUCE

1 CUP HEAVY CREAM       1 CUP WHITE SUGAR
2 TABLESPOONS UNSALTED BUTTER       ½ TEASPOON VANILLA EXTRACT

In a small saucepan heat the cream over very low heat. As soon as it comes to a boil, turn off the heat and let stand, covered, on the burner.

In a small, deep saucepan melt the butter over low heat. Stir in one-third of the sugar, then let it sit for about 30 seconds, until it liquefies slightly. Stir in another ⅓ cup of sugar, then stir constantly for about 3 minutes, until very smooth. Add the rest of the sugar and stir continually until golden brown and beginning to liquefy. Stirring vigorously, pour in a third of the cream. Remove from the heat and, stirring constantly, slowly pour in the rest of the cream.

Return the pan to very low heat and bring to a boil. Boil for 2 minutes, stirring constantly. Be careful since this can easily splatter. Remove from the heat and stir in the vanilla extract. Strain into a sauceboat or large creamer and cool to room temperature. Save any solid bits of caramel in your strainer and add to vanilla ice cream with any leftover caramel sauce to make praline ice cream.

NOTE: If you make this in advance and refrigerate it, you'll have to warm it over very low heat for just a couple of minutes, watching constantly so the sauce doesn't get grainy. It should be room temperature, not hot, so it doesn't melt the ice cream roll.

**MAKES 1⅓ CUPS**

Bundt cakes and coffee are made for each other, and this is no exception. The whole wheat flour makes the cake quite substantial, while the mashed potatoes keep it moist. You can also include coarsely ground ginger Macaroons (see recipe, page 44) in the brown sugar–nut mixture for an unusual but terrific taste and texture.

| | |
|---|---|
| ½ CUP PLUS 6 TABLESPOONS BROWN SUGAR | ½ TEASPOON GROUND GINGER |
| ¾ CUP COARSELY CHOPPED WALNUTS AND/OR PECANS | ½ TEASPOON GROUND CINNAMON |
| 1 CUP WHITE SUGAR | ¼ TEASPOON GROUND CARDAMOM |
| 1½ CUPS UNBLEACHED OR WHITE PRESIFTED ALL-PURPOSE FLOUR | ¼ TEASPOON GROUND CLOVES |
| 1 CUP WHOLE WHEAT FLOUR | ½ CUP UNSALTED BUTTER, AT ROOM TEMPERATURE |
| 1 TEASPOON BAKING SODA | ⅓ CUP MASHED POTATOES |
| 2 TEASPOONS BAKING POWDER | 2 LARGE EGGS PLUS 1 LARGE YOLK |
| ½ TEASPOON SALT | 1 TEASPOON VANILLA EXTRACT |
| | 2 TABLESPOONS MOLASSES |
| | 1 CUP SOUR CREAM |

Toss ½ cup brown sugar with the nuts and set aside.

Mix well the 6 tablespoons brown sugar, the white sugar, flours, baking soda and powder, salt, ginger, cinnamon, cardamom, and cloves and set aside.

Preheat the oven to 350°F. Grease a 9″ or 10″ bundt or tube pan, preferably springform.

Beat together the butter, potatoes, eggs, yolk, vanilla, and molasses until smooth. Beat in, in the following order, one-third of the flour mixture,

½ cup sour cream, half the remaining flour, the remaining sour cream, and the remaining flour.

Spoon half the batter into the pan. Smooth with damp fingers, then bang the pan on the counter once or twice to remove any air. Sprinkle evenly with half the nut and sugar mixture. Repeat both layers. Bake for about 1 hour, until a skewer comes out clean. Cool the cake in the pan on a rack for 15 minutes. Then, running a knife around the edges of the cake if necessary, turn out onto a plate. Turn back over onto the rack and cool completely.

"Parkin" refers to any British gingerbread in which oatmeal replaces some of the flour. Two hundred years ago gingerbread cookies were eaten; later, the lighter cakes were developed. This was the interim version, a cross between cookies and cake. Parkin biscuits (ginger oatmeal cookies) are more popular in Scotland, while this cake is more common in northern England. Authentic versions can contain mutton fat, lard, buttermilk, figs, almonds, or candied fruit, so you have a lot of leeway if you want to experiment.

While this is often baked a week ahead of time and left to mellow in an airtight tin, it's also eaten hot, topped with applesauce.

½ CUP UNSALTED BUTTER

6 TABLESPOONS TREACLE OR
  MOLASSES

¾ CUP BROWN SUGAR

1½ TEASPOONS GROUND GINGER

1 TEASPOON GROUND NUTMEG

½ TEASPOON GROUND ALLSPICE

1½ CUPS UNBLEACHED OR WHITE
  PRESIFTED ALL-PURPOSE FLOUR

2 LARGE EGGS, LIGHTLY BEATEN

2½ CUPS ROLLED OATS

½ CUP BEER

WHIPPED CREAM

Preheat the oven to 350°F. Grease and flour an 8″ square baking pan.

In a small saucepan melt the butter over low heat, then stir in the molasses and brown sugar. Scrape out into a large bowl and stir in the ginger, nutmeg, and allspice. Gradually beat in the flour, then the eggs. Then fold in, in the following order, one third of the oats, half the beer, half the remaining oats, the remaining beer, and the remaining oats.

Pour the batter into the pan and bake for 45 minutes. Cool, cut into 16 squares, and serve with whipped cream.

**MAKES 16 SERVINGS**

Traditional pound cake is made with a pound each of sugar, flour, and butter. This gingered version is delicious sliced and topped with ice cream and fruit sauce. It's also perfect for trifle or topped with any other custard or pudding. Toasted pound cake, like ordinary gingerbread cake, is a breakfast treat, especially when spread with thick fruit preserves.

½ TEASPOON SALT

1 TEASPOON GROUND GINGER

1 TEASPOON GROUND CINNAMON

¾ TEASPOON GROUND CLOVES

¼ TEASPOON GROUND MACE

1 POUND (2 CUPS) UNSALTED
   BUTTER

1 POUND (2 CUPS) BROWN SUGAR

3 TABLESPOONS MOLASSES

1 TEASPOON VANILLA EXTRACT

8 LARGE EGGS

1 POUND (ABOUT 3¼ CUPS)
   UNBLEACHED OR WHITE PRESIFTED
   ALL-PURPOSE FLOUR

Preheat the oven to 350°F. Grease a 10″ tube or bundt cake pan. Mix together the salt, ginger, cinnamon, cloves, and mace and set aside.

Melt the butter in a small saucepan. Remove from the heat and beat in the sugar and molasses. Scrape into a bowl and cool until just warm to the touch.

Beat in the spice mixture and vanilla, then the eggs, 2 at a time. Beat in the flour, a third at a time, until smooth.

Pour the batter into the cake pan and bake for about 1¼ hours, until a skewer comes out clean. If the top begins to get too brown, cover with foil. It's not a problem if the top cracks, since that will be the bottom of the cake. Cool the cake in the pan for 30 minutes, then turn out and cool completely.

**MAKES 16 SERVINGS**

# GINGERBREAD AND LEMON CHECKERBOARD CAKE WITH MERINGUE FROSTING

Lemon and gingerbread are made for each other, and this cake is always a favorite. It's easiest to use a checkerboard cake pan for this recipe and follow the manufacturer's directions for pouring in the batter. I've discovered a way to attach the layers without any intrusive frosting between them. That makes the cake even more magical to children and adults alike. If you don't have a checkerboard pan, you can always make two thin layers of each batter, cooling and attaching them the same way as below.

1 CUP UNSALTED BUTTER

1 ½ CUPS WHITE SUGAR

6 LARGE EGGS

1 ½ TABLESPOONS BAKING POWDER

1 ½ TEASPOONS SALT

4 CUPS UNBLEACHED OR WHITE
   PRESIFTED ALL-PURPOSE FLOUR

1 CUP MILK

½ CUP MOLASSES

1 ¼ TEASPOONS GROUND GINGER

1 ¼ TEASPOONS GROUND CINNAMON

¼ TEASPOON GROUND NUTMEG

¼ TEASPOON GROUND CLOVES

1 ½ TABLESPOONS GRATED LEMON
   RIND, PLUS 2 TABLESPOONS
   JUICE

1 RECIPE BROWN SUGAR MERINGUE
   FROSTING (PAGE 63)

Preheat the oven to 350°F. Grease and flour 3 cake pans.

Beat the butter until smooth. Beat in 1 cup of the sugar, then the eggs, 2 at a time, until smooth. Stir in the baking powder and salt. Beat in 2 cups of the flour, then the milk, then the remaining flour. Pour half the batter into a second bowl.

To make the gingerbread batter, beat the molasses, ginger, cinnamon, nutmeg, and cloves into one bowl of batter. To make the lemon batter, beat the lemon rind and juice into the other bowl.

Spoon the batter into the 3 cake pans according to the manufacturer's instructions. Two pans should have two rings of gingerbread with one of lemon in between; the third should have two rings of lemon with one of gingerbread in between. As you fill each pan, hold the divider down firmly or some of the batter may run under it. Make sure the height of all the rings is even before you remove the divider.

Bake the layers for about 25 minutes, until a skewer comes out clean. Turn one of the layers with two gingerbread rings out onto a large piece of foil set on a baking sheet. Turn the layer with two lemon rings out onto a plate, then slide it onto the first layer. Turn out the third layer and slide it atop the first two. Place two upside-down dinner plates on top of the cake to weight it. Cool completely, then carefully remove the dinner plates. The layers will now be fused together.

Preheat the oven to 450°. Make the meringue. Frost the cake with the meringue, swirling it into a decorative pattern.

Place the baking sheet in the oven and bake for 5 to 10 minutes, until lightly browned, with dark brown peaks. Immediately cut off any excess meringue on the foil with a sharp knife. Let the cake and meringue cool completely, then carefully peel off the foil.

**MAKES 12 SERVINGS**

# BROWN SUGAR MERINGUE FROSTING

½ TEASPOON CREAM OF TARTAR          6 LARGE EGG WHITES

1 ½ TEASPOONS VANILLA EXTRACT       ½ CUP BROWN SUGAR

Whisk the cream of tartar, vanilla, and egg whites until the mixture holds soft peaks. Whisk in the brown sugar, in 4 parts, then continue to whisk until it holds stiff peaks.

Making upside-down cake is more of a technique than a separate recipe. You can also make pear, apple, or peach upside-down cake the same way, using either fresh or canned fruit.

1 RECIPE BASIC GINGERBREAD CAKE BATTER (PAGE 52)

¼ CUP UNSALTED BUTTER

1 CUP BROWN SUGAR

8 CANNED PINEAPPLE SLICES, DRAINED WELL AND HALVED

Make the cake batter and set it aside. Preheat the oven to 350°F.

In an 8″ square cake pan melt the butter over very low heat. Stir in the brown sugar until crumbly and well mixed. Remove the pan from the heat and tilt it to cover the bottom evenly. If necessary, pat the sugar mixture out with a wooden spoon.

Arrange the pineapple in one layer. Spoon in the batter, being careful not to dislodge the fruit. Bake for about 45 minutes, until a skewer comes out clean. Cool the cake in the pan on a rack for 15 minutes, then turn it out onto a serving plate. If any of the pineapple or sugar topping sticks to the pan, just pat it back into place on the cake.

**MAKES 9 SERVINGS**

While this is not a true génoise, it is inspired by that French classic. This is a very delicate cake, requiring a delicate filling and frosting. I like to create a grand strawberry or peach shortcake. Sandwich sliced fresh fruit with just a little whipped cream between the layers. Decoratively pipe out whipped cream onto the top of the cake, leaving the sides uncovered. You can also fill the layers with plain whipped cream, then cover the cake with a thin dark-chocolate glaze. I use the chocolate cream glaze found in Rose Levy Beranbaum's superb book, *The Cake Bible.*

6 LARGE EGGS

1 CUP WHITE SUGAR

¼ TEASPOON VANILLA EXTRACT

¼ TEASPOON ALMOND EXTRACT

1 ¼ TEASPOONS GROUND GINGER

1 ¼ TEASPOONS GROUND CINNAMON

1 TEASPOON GROUND CLOVES

6 TABLESPOONS UNSALTED BUTTER,
  MELTED AND COOLED

1 ¼ CUPS CAKE FLOUR

Preheat the oven to 350°F. Grease and flour two 9″ round cake pans. Whisk together the eggs, sugar, and vanilla and almond extracts, then beat for 7 or 8 minutes, until very thick and almost white. Beat the ginger, cinnamon, cloves, and butter into the egg mixture. Gently fold in half the flour. Fold in the remaining flour just until completely moistened.

Pour the batter into the cake pans. Lightly bang the pans on the counter a couple of times and rotate to even out the tops. Bake for about 25 minutes, until a skewer comes out clean. Quickly run a sharp knife around the sides of the cake layers and turn out onto a wire rack. Cool to room temperature, then add filling and frosting suggested at beginning of recipe.

**MAKES 10 SERVINGS**

Until recently I had forgotten how good Baked Alaska is, since the last time I had it was in 1966 when I was fourteen years old. It was the highlight of the end-of-summer-camp banquet, and we spent the entire night back in our bunks trying to figure out why the ice cream didn't melt under the hot meringue. As I recall, we finally just threw up our hands and assumed it was witchcraft. This is one of the few recipes where you're better off with less expensive, not premium, ice cream, since it retains its shape better. Use a simple flavor, such as vanilla, strawberry, coffee, chocolate, or praline, not one that will overshadow the cake and meringue. While the directions below are long, every step is very simple. The cake can be baked and the ice cream frozen in the cake pan up to a day ahead, so all you have to do at the last minute is make the meringue, put the Baked Alaska together, and brown it.

| | |
|---|---|
| 1 ¼ TEASPOONS GROUND GINGER | 2 TABLESPOONS HONEY |
| 1 ¼ TEASPOONS GROUND CINNAMON | 2 TABLESPOONS MOLASSES |
| ¼ TEASPOON GROUND CLOVES | 3 LARGE EGGS |
| ¼ TEASPOON GROUND NUTMEG | 2 CUPS UNBLEACHED OR WHITE |
| 1 TEASPOON BAKING SODA | PRESIFTED ALL-PURPOSE FLOUR |
| ½ TEASPOON SALT | 1 QUART ICE CREAM |
| ½ CUP UNSALTED BUTTER | 1 RECIPE BROWN SUGAR MERINGUE |
| ½ CUP BROWN SUGAR | (PAGE 67) |

Line an 8″ square baking pan with foil, pressing it well into the corners without tearing it. Lightly grease and set aside. Mix together the ginger, cinnamon, cloves, nutmeg, baking soda, and salt; set aside.

In a small saucepan melt the butter, then stir in the sugar, honey, and molasses. Scrape into a bowl, then stir in the spice mixture and cool slightly. Preheat the oven to 350°F.

When the butter mixture is just warm to the touch, beat in the eggs. Fold in the flour just until completely moistened. Pour the batter into the pan, making sure it fills the corners, then even out the top with dampened hands. Bake for about 1 hour, until a skewer comes out clean. Turn the cake out of the pan, peel off the foil, then turn the cake back over so the top side is up. Cool completely.

Remove the ice cream from the freezer. If you don't have a 7″ square cake pan, crumble up clean foil and place around the insides of the washed 8″ cake pan to create one. Line either pan with waxed paper. As soon as the ice cream is malleable, pack it into the pan. Place the pan and 6 dessert plates in the freezer until very cold.

Cut the cooled cake into 6 rectangles, then cut off as much of the top as necessary to even it. Hollow out the center of each piece to make a rectangle ½″ deep. Leave ¼″ to ½″ of cake around the sides of the rectangle. Cut the very cold ice cream into rectangles which will fit into the cut-out hollows in the cake. The ice cream will come up over the top of the cake. Freeze the cake with the ice cream for 15 minutes.

Preheat the oven to 450°F. Make the meringue. Remove the cakes from the freezer and place on a foil-covered baking sheet. Quickly and generously slather each with meringue. Bake for 5 minutes, watching carefully. As soon as the meringue is lightly browned with dark peaks, remove and serve.

**MAKES 6 BAKED ALASKAS**

# BROWN SUGAR MERINGUE

¾ TEASPOON CREAM OF TARTAR          9 LARGE EGG WHITES

1 TABLESPOON VANILLA EXTRACT          ¼ CUP BROWN SUGAR

Whisk the cream of tartar, vanilla, and egg whites together until the mixture holds soft peaks. Whisk in the brown sugar, then continue to whisk until it holds stiff peaks.

This is a popular cake in both The Netherlands and its former colony, Indonesia. Its name is Dutch for "bacon cake," because when sliced it resembles a strip of bacon. Although it's time-consuming to make, it actually requires very little work and can easily be made while you're doing something else in the kitchen.

This cake must be made at least two days ahead. The taste is so sharp and the texture so rubbery the first day, you'll think it's a disaster. The second day, the taste has mellowed and the texture seems lighter. On the third day, the chocolate taste emerges in the gingerbread layers; suddenly, the cake's a masterpiece. It remains in perfect shape for another two days if tightly wrapped in foil. For a larger cake, double the recipe and make twelve layers instead of six.

1 ¼ TEASPOONS GROUND GINGER

1 ¼ TEASPOONS GROUND CINNAMON

1 TEASPOON GROUND CLOVES

3 TABLESPOONS UNSWEETENED COCOA POWDER, SIEVED TO RID OF LUMPS

1 ¼ CUPS CAKE FLOUR

7 LARGE EGGS, SEPARATED, PLUS 2 WHITES

¾ CUP UNSALTED BUTTER, AT ROOM TEMPERATURE, PLUS 5 TABLESPOONS, MELTED

1 CUP WHITE SUGAR

1 TEASPOON VANILLA EXTRACT

Mix together the ginger, cinnamon, cloves, cocoa, and half the flour (⅝ cup) and set aside.

Beat the egg yolks until completely broken up. Add the ¾ cup of room temperature butter, sugar, and vanilla to the yolks, then beat for about 5 minutes, until smooth, thick, and pale yellow.

Preheat the oven to 300°F. Grease a 9″ or 9½″ springform pan. Beat the egg whites until stiff. Fold into the yolk mixture, half at a time, just until incorporated. Pour out half into a second bowl. Gently fold the flour and spice mixture into one bowl, the remaining flour (⅝ cup) into the other.

Spoon a third of the gingerbread batter into the bottom of the pan. Smooth it out with the back of a spoon until you have an even, very thin layer. Bake until a skewer in the center of the cake comes out clean, about 15 minutes. Remove the cake from the oven and brush gently but thoroughly with some of the melted butter. Spoon in a third of the white batter, quickly spreading it with the back of a spoon to form an even layer. Bake until a skewer in just the top layer comes out clean, about 18 minutes, then brush with butter.

Continue adding layers until the batter is used up. Each layer takes a few minutes longer to bake than the previous one. After adding the final layer, bake until a skewer inserted to the bottom of the cake comes out clean, about 30 minutes.

Place the cake on a wire rack, then carefully run a knife around the sides. Remove the sides of the pan. Turn the cake over to remove the pan bottom, then revert until it's top side up again. Let the cake cool to room temperature on the rack, then wrap in foil and store at room temperature for at least 2 days before serving.

**MAKES 8 SERVINGS**

# COCONUT CAKE WITH MOCHA FROSTING

This cake has an old-fashioned feeling, as if you'd expect to find it in a wonderful little bakery which has been in business for fifty years. You can use almost any flavor frosting if you prefer it to mocha. Your favorite recipes for banana, vanilla, lemon, or milk or dark chocolate frosting would all be delicious. I always make extra toasted coconut, since I invariably find myself snacking on it all day long. If you can find toasted flaked coconut at a health food store or fruit stand, it's just as good as homemade.

1 ½ CUPS SWEETENED FLAKED
    COCONUT
1 TABLESPOON BAKING POWDER
½ TEASPOON SALT
1 TEASPOON GROUND GINGER
1 TEASPOON GROUND CINNAMON
1 TEASPOON GROUND CLOVES
½ TEASPOON GROUND CARDAMOM

¾ CUP UNSALTED BUTTER, AT ROOM
    TEMPERATURE
4 LARGE EGGS, SEPARATED
1 CUP BROWN SUGAR
½ CUP MOLASSES
3 CUPS CAKE FLOUR
1 ¼ CUPS MILK
1 RECIPE MOCHA FROSTING
   (PAGE 71)

Preheat the oven to 350°F. Grease three 8″ round cake pans. Spread ½ cup of the coconut on a baking sheet and toast it in the oven for 5 minutes, until lightly browned. Set aside to cool. Keep the oven on.

Mix together the baking powder, salt, ginger, cinnamon, cloves, and cardamom and set aside.

Whisk the butter and egg yolks together until smooth. Whisk in the sugar and molasses, then the spice mixture. Gently stir in, in the following order, 1 cup flour, half the milk, 1 cup flour, the remaining milk, and the remaining flour. It's all right if not all the flour is moistened at this point.

Beat the egg whites until stiff, then gently fold into the cake batter, half at a time. Fold in the untoasted coconut.

Divide the batter among the 3 cake pans. Bake for 20 minutes, until a skewer comes out clean. Run a knife around the sides of the cakes, then turn the pans over onto a wire rack. The cakes will fall right out.

Cool the cake layers completely while making the frosting. Place one cake layer on a serving plate. Slide 4 strips of waxed paper under the cake to keep the rim of the plate clean. Spread on just enough frosting to cover the top of the layer evenly. Add a second cake layer and frost the top. Top with the third layer and use the remaining frosting to cover the top and sides of the entire cake. Sprinkle the top and sides of the cake with the toasted coconut, gently pressing it into the frosting with your fingers. Remove the waxed paper before serving.

**Makes 10 servings**

## MOCHA FROSTING

1 ¼ CUPS UNSALTED BUTTER

2 ½ CUPS CONFECTIONERS' SUGAR

⅓ ½ CUP PLUS 2 TABLESPOONS STRONG BLACK COFFEE

5 TABLESPOONS UNSWEETENED COCOA POWDER, SIEVED TO RID OF LUMPS

Beat the butter and sugar together until smooth, then beat in the coffee and cocoa. Refrigerate briefly if runny.

# CHOCOLATE NUT TORTE

Tortes are elegant European cakes, usually complete without any icing or with just a simple glaze. Ground nuts often replace some of the flour, adding interesting texture and richness. In this cake, the fresh ginger complements the chocolate beautifully. I prefer the cake plain, but you can serve it with Caramel Sauce (see recipe, page 57) or excellent store-bought hot fudge sauce, if you prefer. This is the perfect finish to a perfect dinner party. Serve with fresh berries, coffee, and a glass of port or good sauterne.

1 TABLESPOON GROUND GINGERSNAPS OR GINGER GRAHAM CRACKER CRUMBS (PAGE 25 OR 128)

½ CUP SHELLED HAZELNUTS, WALNUTS, OR BLANCHED ALMONDS

¼ CUP UNBLEACHED OR WHITE PRESIFTED ALL-PURPOSE FLOUR

¼ POUND GRATED BITTERSWEET CHOCOLATE

½ CUP UNSALTED BUTTER

½ CUP WHITE SUGAR

½ CUP BROWN SUGAR

1 TABLESPOON GRATED FRESH GINGER

¾ TEASPOON GROUND CLOVES

½ TEASPOON GROUND CINNAMON

⅛ TEASPOON GROUND NUTMEG

PINCH OF SALT

2 TABLESPOONS MOLASSES

1 TABLESPOON UNSWEETENED COCOA POWDER, SIEVED TO RID OF LUMPS

1 TABLESPOON ORANGE OR COFFEE LIQUEUR

5 LARGE EGGS, SEPARATED

Preheat the oven to 375°F. Butter an 8″ round springform pan. Line the bottom with waxed paper or parchment, then butter the paper. Dust the inside of the pan with the gingersnap or graham cracker crumbs. Pour out any excess. Refrigerate the pan until you're ready to use it.

Place the nuts on a baking sheet and toast for 10 minutes, shaking the pan occasionally, until browned all over. Don't turn the oven off when you remove the nuts. If you're using hazelnuts, rub briskly with a towel to remove the brown skin. Grind the nuts with 1 tablespoon of the flour in a nut grinder or food processor, using on-off pulses, until fine but not pasty.

Melt the chocolate and butter together over low heat, then scrape into a bowl. Beat in both sugars, then the ginger, cloves, cinnamon, nutmeg, salt, molasses, cocoa, and liqueur. Beat in the yolks, one at a time. Stir in the nuts and flour. Beat the egg whites until stiff, then fold into the batter.

Spoon the batter into the pan, being careful not to dislodge the crumbs. Rotate the pan to smooth the top. Bake for about 80 minutes, until a skewer comes out clean. The top will be very brown. Place the pan on a rack and cool for 15 minutes. Run a knife around the sides of the cake, then remove the sides of the pan. Turn the cake over onto a plate and peel the paper off the bottom. Turn right side up and cool completely on the rack.

**MAKES 10 SERVINGS**

This is very rich but still quite delicate. The white chocolate comes through as a lovely, sweet, lingering aftertaste rather than being over-powering. You can serve the cake without any icing, or you can top each slice with Caramel Sauce (see recipe, page 57) or fresh berries and whipped cream.

| | |
|---|---|
| 5 LARGE EGGS, SEPARATED | ⅔ CUP UNBLEACHED OR WHITE |
| ½ CUP BROWN SUGAR | PRESIFTED ALL-PURPOSE FLOUR |
| 1 ¼ TEASPOONS GROUND GINGER | ½ POUND WHITE CHOCOLATE |
| 1 ¼ TEASPOONS GROUND CINNAMON | ⅔ CUP GROUND WALNUTS, HALFWAY |
| ½ TEASPOON GROUND NUTMEG | BETWEEN COARSE AND FINE |

Grease and flour a 9″ or 9½″ round cake pan, preferably springform. Beat the egg yolks and sugar in a large bowl until smooth. Beat in the ginger, cinnamon, and nutmeg, then the flour.

Melt the chocolate and slowly add it to the batter, constantly beating. The batter will become very sticky and difficult to work with at this point. Fold in the nuts.

Preheat the oven to 350°F. Beat the egg whites until stiff. You're now going to beat most of the whites into the batter just to lighten it, so it's all right if the batter doesn't increase in volume yet. Beat in one-fifth of the egg whites with a wooden spoon or other strong implement (not a rubber spatula). Beat in another fifth completely, then another fifth. Carefully fold in half the remaining whites. It's all right if there are some white streaks. Fold in the rest of the whites just until there are no more white streaks in the batter.

Scrape the batter into the cake pan, and bake for about 30 minutes, until a skewer inserted in the center comes out clean. Cool the pan on a rack for 15 minutes. Run a knife around the sides of the cake and remove the pan.

**MAKES 10 SERVINGS**

It's the contrast between the two elements of this cake that makes it wonderful. The spiciness in the gingerbread cuts the richness of the cheesecake, while the creaminess of the cheesecake moistens the dense, intense gingerbread. This cake is equally appropriate for both formal and casual family dinners. It can be made up to two days ahead and refrigerated or can be frozen for up to two months.

1 TEASPOON GROUND GINGER

1 TEASPOON GROUND CINNAMON

¼ TEASPOON GROUND NUTMEG

⅛ TEASPOON GROUND CLOVES

¼ TEASPOON SALT

1 ½ TEASPOONS BAKING SODA

1 POUND (2 CUPS) CREAM CHEESE,
   AT ROOM TEMPERATURE

½ TEASPOON VANILLA EXTRACT

4 LARGE EGGS

½ CUP PLUS 2 TABLESPOONS WHITE
   SUGAR

¼ CUP DICED UNSALTED BUTTER, AT
   ROOM TEMPERATURE

½ CUP BROWN SUGAR

¼ CUP MOLASSES

1 CUP UNBLEACHED OR WHITE
   PRESIFTED ALL-PURPOSE FLOUR

Mix together the ginger, cinnamon, nutmeg, cloves, salt, and baking soda and set aside.

Beat the cream cheese, preferably with an electric mixer, until smooth. Beat in the vanilla, then 2 eggs, then the white sugar, completely incorporating each ingredient before adding the next. Remove half the cream cheese mixture and refrigerate it.

Melt the butter in a small saucepan. Stir in the brown sugar and molasses, then scrape into a large bowl. Beat in the spice mixture and the remaining 2 eggs. Stir in the flour in 2 batches. Refrigerate for at least 20 minutes.

Preheat the oven to 350°F., and grease a 9″ or 9½″ round springform pan. With a tablespoon, drop half the gingerbread batter in lumps, lines, or strings onto the bottom of the pan. Fill the spaces with half the chilled cheesecake mixture. Very gently cover the cheesecake lumps with the rest of the gingerbread. Fill the new spaces with the remaining chilled cheesecake. Using the flat edge of a knife, swirl the pan contents to make a pretty pattern. Be careful not to mix the 2 batters. Gently pour on the room temperature cheesecake.

Bake for about 50 minutes, until the top of the cake begins to crack in the center. The cake may be lumpy since the gingerbread rises and the cheesecake sinks, but it's still nice-looking. Cool to room temperature, then remove the sides of the cake pan. Refrigerate for at least 3 hours. Serve cold.

**MAKES 8 SERVINGS**

# VANILLA "SWISS WALNUT" CHEESECAKE IN A GINGER CRUST

I usually prefer baked cheesecake to the unbaked variety, but this is irresistibly rich, smooth, and creamy. The addition of the chocolate-covered nuts in this cake was inspired by a friend's favorite ice cream flavor, vanilla Swiss almond. You can refrigerate the cake for up to two days. After that, the crust gets slightly soggy, but if you like a moist crust, that's not a problem.

1¾ CUPS FINELY GROUND
   GINGERSNAPS OR GINGER
   GRAHAM CRACKER CRUMBS
   (PAGE 25 OR 128)
¼ CUP UNSALTED BUTTER, MELTED
1 OUNCE SEMISWEET OR
   BITTERSWEET CHOCOLATE, PLUS 1
   TABLESPOON GRATED
⅔ CUP ROUGHLY CHOPPED WALNUTS

½ CUP MILK
1 ENVELOPE UNFLAVORED GELATIN
3 LARGE EGGS, SEPARATED
1 CUP BROWN SUGAR
1 POUND (2 CUPS) CREAM CHEESE,
   AT ROOM TEMPERATURE
1 TEASPOON VANILLA EXTRACT
1 CUP HEAVY CREAM

Preheat the oven to 350°F. Place the gingersnap or ginger graham crumbs in an ungreased 9"-x-2" springform cake pan. Pour in the melted butter and stir together with a fork until all the crumbs are moistened. Press out the mixture with your fingers to form an even crust on the bottom and sides of the pan. Bake for 10 minutes, then set aside to cool completely.

Melt the 1 ounce chocolate. Stir in the nuts until they're completely chocolate-coated. Spread them out on a sheet of foil or waxed paper, making sure the nuts don't stick together. Place in the freezer.

Pour the milk into a small saucepan. Whisk in the gelatin until well mixed. Whisk in the egg yolks and ¾ cup of the brown sugar. Turn the heat to low and, stirring almost constantly, cook until the mixture coats the back of a spoon, about 8 minutes. Take the pan off the burner and set aside.

Beat the cream cheese until smooth, then beat in the vanilla. Constantly beating, slowly pour in the gelatin mixture. Beat until smooth. If there are any lumps, whisk to break them up. Set aside. Beat the egg whites until frothy, then add the remaining ¼ cup brown sugar. Beat until stiff, then fold into the cream cheese until completely incorporated. Beat the cream until stiff, then fold that in. Pour into the crust.

Remove the nuts from the freezer. Breaking up any that have stuck together, drop them into the cream cheese, distributing them evenly. Refrigerate the cake until very cold, about 4 hours. Sprinkle the grated chocolate over the top.

You can use almost any cake batter to make cupcakes. I prefer more delicate cupcakes, so I use honey in these rather than molasses. Don't overfill the cups with the batter, since cupcakes rise. The closer the batter to the top of the cup, the larger the overhanging portion of the baked cupcake.

½ CUP UNSALTED BUTTER

½ CUP BROWN SUGAR

½ CUP HONEY

2 CUPS UNBLEACHED OR WHITE
   PRESIFTED ALL-PURPOSE FLOUR

1 ¼ TEASPOONS GROUND GINGER

1 ¼ TEASPOONS GROUND CINNAMON

¼ TEASPOON GROUND CLOVES

¼ TEASPOON GROUND NUTMEG

1 TEASPOON BAKING SODA

½ TEASPOON SALT

3 LARGE EGGS

½ CUP COARSELY CHOPPED WALNUTS
   OR PECANS

½ CUP FINELY CHOPPED CANDIED
   GINGER

Preheat the oven to 375°F. Grease 12 muffin cups. Melt the butter and pour into a small bowl. Stir in the sugar and honey and cool slightly.

In a large bowl mix together well the flour, ground ginger, cinnamon, cloves, nutmeg, baking soda, and salt and set aside.

When the butter is just warm to the touch, beat in the eggs. Stir into the flour mixture only until the flour is moistened. Fold in the nuts and candied ginger. Spoon into the muffin cups. It's all right if the mixture looks lumpy in the pan. Bake for 20 to 25 minutes, until a skewer inserted into the center of a cupcake comes out clean. Turn out of the cups and cool on a wire rack.

**MAKES 12 CUPCAKES**

This is my favorite cupcake—delicate, slightly sticky, and sweet without being cloying. If you can find exotic bananas, such as monsano or any ladyfinger variety, they make intensely flavored, fine-textured banana cupcakes. Richardson's Seaside Banana Gardens in La Conchita, California, sells over forty different banana varieties by mail order. Call or write Doug Richardson and ask him to recommend a particular banana or order a sampler pack of four or five varieties; it will be a revelation. The address and phone number are 6823 Santa Barbara Avenue, Ventura, CA 93001; (805) 643-4061.

¾ CUP COARSELY GROUND WALNUTS OR PECANS

1 CUP GRATED COCONUT

1 TABLESPOON FRESH GINGER

1½ CUPS (APPROXIMATELY 3) VERY RIPE BANANAS

½ CUP DARK BROWN SUGAR

3 LARGE EGGS, SEPARATED

1 TEASPOON BAKING SODA

½ TEASPOON SALT

1 TEASPOON GROUND CINNAMON

¼ TEASPOON GROUND ALLSPICE

¼ TEASPOON GROUND NUTMEG

¾ CUP BUTTERSCOTCH CHIPS

¾ CUP UNBLEACHED OR WHITE PRESIFTED ALL-PURPOSE FLOUR

Preheat the oven to 350°F. Place the nuts and coconut on a baking sheet and toast for about 5 minutes, until lightly browned. Remove from the oven and set aside to cool.

Turn the oven to 400°. Grease 12 muffin cups. Roughly chop the ginger if you're going to use a food processor; finely mince or put it through a garlic press if you'll be beating the batter by hand.

Process or mash and beat the bananas until smooth. Beat or process in the sugar and egg yolks, then the ginger, baking soda, salt, cinnamon, allspice, and nutmeg until smooth. If using the processor, turn the batter out into a bowl. Fold the nuts, coconut, and butterscotch chips into the batter. Gently fold in the flour. It's not a problem if you still see a few streaks of dry flour.

Beat the egg whites until stiff. Fold half the whites into the batter, then the second half. It's better to have a few streaks of egg white showing than to overmix. Spoon the mixture into the muffin cups. Each cup should be completely filled.

Bake the cupcakes for about 20 to 25 minutes, until a tester comes out clean. Cool the cupcakes in the pan for about 15 minutes. Then cut around the sides of the cupcakes if necessary and turn out onto a wire rack. Eat as soon as they've cooled to room temperature or within a couple of hours.

**MAKES 12 CUPCAKES**

❄·❄·❄·❄
**A**lthough I admit a certain bias, I'm convinced that almost any dessert could use a touch of gingerbread. This chapter is a catchall for every dessert that isn't a cookie or cake: pies, pastries, puddings, ice creams, fruit desserts, and any-
❄·❄·❄·❄· thing else I thought needed spicing up. My favorites are the recipes for gingerbread shells, including "tacos," tarts, cream puffs, and even Italian cannoli. Gingersnap, gingerbread cookie, or ginger graham cracker crumbs highlight other desserts like baked apple stuffings or piecrusts. These crumbs make almost any dessert more exciting if you use them as a replacement for bread crumbs or regular graham cracker crumbs.

As I've said in previous chapters, the main thing to remember when adding gingerbread flavorings to usually plain recipes is to taste constantly. If the unbaked dish is just slightly spicier than you like, when baked it will be perfect.

This very pretty dessert is typical of the California and new southwestern cuisines. These are just larger tuile cookies in a different shape. You can, of course, fill them with whatever your taste and imagination dictate. Dollops of chocolate or strawberry mousse would be terrific. Fill them at the last minute, or they become soggy. In polite company I eat these with a fork; if I have any left over I just pick them up with my fingers and eat them taco-style.

3 LARGE EGG WHITES

½ CUP WHITE SUGAR

1 TABLESPOON HONEY

2 TABLESPOONS MOLASSES

½ TEASPOON VANILLA EXTRACT

1 TEASPOON GROUND GINGER

1 TEASPOON GROUND CINNAMON

½ TEASPOON GROUND NUTMEG

6 TABLESPOONS UNSALTED BUTTER,
   MELTED AND COOLED

½ CUP UNBLEACHED OR WHITE
   PRESIFTED ALL-PURPOSE FLOUR

½ CUP FINELY CHOPPED BLANCHED
   ALMONDS

2 CUPS WHIPPED CREAM,
   SWEETENED OR NOT DEPENDING
   ON PREFERENCE

2½ CUPS FRESH BERRIES, HALVED IF
   LARGE

Preheat the oven to 325°F. Grease your baking sheets. Whisk together the egg whites, sugar, honey, molasses, and vanilla. Whisk in the ginger, cinnamon, and nutmeg, then the butter. Then beat or whisk in the flour and nuts just until moistened.

Drop by large heaping tablespoons at least 4″ apart onto the baking sheet. There should be only 3 cookies per sheet. With the back of a spoon, spread the cookies out into even 5″ circles. Bake one sheet at a time, or at 5 minute intervals, since the cookies must be removed from the baking sheet as soon as possible. They take about 13 to 15 minutes to brown around the edges. Cool the cookies on the sheet for 1 minute, until a spatula detaching them doesn't tear them.

Pick up one cookie and place it, top side down, on your counter. Set a 1″ cylinder, such as a cannoli tube or wooden dowel, on one side of the cookie, parallel to the diameter. Pull up the opposite side of the cookie and drape over the cylinder to create the traditional taco-shell shape. As soon as the "taco shells" are stiff, which should only take about 5 minutes, remove them to a wire rack to cool completely. Make the rest of the cookies, greasing the baking sheet well before each batch.

Just before serving, spoon or pipe 2 tablespoons of whipped cream inside each shell. Gently press 3 tablespoons of berries into the whipped cream, then top with another tablespoon of cream. Serve at once.

**MAKES 10 "TACOS"**

In this recipe the gingersnaps not only add flavor to the stuffing, but they also thicken the surrounding syrup, creating a delicious sauce.

2 TABLESPOONS FINELY CHOPPED
   WALNUTS
3 TABLESPOONS BROWN SUGAR
¼ CUP GROUND GINGERSNAPS OR
   MACAROON CRUMBS (PAGE 25
   OR 44)

2 GRANNY SMITH OR OTHER TART
   APPLES (APPROXIMATELY 8
   OUNCES EACH)
¼ CUP COLD WATER
1 TEASPOON UNSALTED BUTTER

Preheat the oven to 400°F. Mix together the walnuts, sugar, and all but 1 tablespoon of the cookie crumbs in a 15-ounce oval baking dish or one just large enough to hold both apples without touching. Core the apples, without breaking through the bottom, making 1″-diameter holes.

Stuff the apples tightly with some of the nut mixture. Place the apples amid the remaining nut mixture in the baking dish. Cut a circle around the apples, just through the skin 1″ from the top, to prevent them from splitting. Carefully spoon the cold water into the dish around the apples. Dot the top of the apples with the butter.

Bake the apples for about 30 minutes, until tender when pierced with a toothpick. Using a slotted spoon, remove the apples to individual plates. Spoon the pan juices over them. Just before serving, sprinkle with the reserved cookie crumbs. Serve hot or cold.

**MAKES 2 BAKED APPLES**

Tartlet shells turn ordinary desserts into elegant party fare. Fill with fresh or poached fruit and whipped cream, slightly softened ice cream, or any kind of mousse. Kids love the fact that they can pick these up and eat them with their fingers. You can also use this dough to make tiny tartlet shells for petits fours. It's best to fill the shells at the last minute, or they'll soften; however, in some desserts, such as banana cream pie, that's not a problem. The unfilled shells can be stored in an airtight container or tightly wrapped in foil for up to two days.

1 TEASPOON GROUND GINGER

1 TEASPOON GROUND CINNAMON

¼ TEASPOON GROUND NUTMEG

¼ TEASPOON GROUND CLOVES

½ TEASPOON SALT

½ CUP UNSALTED BUTTER

⅓ CUP MOLASSES

⅓ CUP BROWN SUGAR

1 LARGE EGG

2 CUPS UNBLEACHED OR WHITE
PRESIFTED ALL-PURPOSE FLOUR

1 RECIPE CHOCOLATE CREAM FILLING
(PAGE 87)

Mix together the ginger, cinnamon, nutmeg, cloves, and salt and set aside.

Melt the butter in a small saucepan. Remove from the heat and stir in the molasses and sugar. Scrape into a bowl. Stir in the spice mixture, then beat in the egg until smooth. Stir in the flour, about ½ cup at a time, just until completely moistened.

Turn the dough out onto a piece of foil or plastic wrap and pat into a 6″ square. Wrap the square tightly and refrigerate it for 3 hours to 2 weeks.

When you're ready to make the tarts, preheat the oven to 350°F. Butter 24 fluted tartlet tins or brioche molds, each about 1½″ to 2″ deep and 3″ across the top, or the underside of 1½″-deep muffin tins. Set the individual tins on a baking sheet.

Roll out one-quarter of the dough at a time, keeping the rest refrigerated, on a floured board with a floured rolling pin, until ⅛" thick. Cut out six 4" circles, rerolling scraps if necessary. Press the dough into the tartlet tins, repairing any tears by pressing the dough together or patching it with a scrap of extra dough. If you're using the muffin tins, drape the dough over them and pinch together any excess to make 4 to 6 evenly spaced points. Form the remaining shells.

Bake for 10 minutes, then turn out onto a rack. They'll fall out of the tartlet tins easily. To loosen from muffin tins, wearing a glove or with a pot holder, give each of the shells a slight twist. Turn the tin over and they'll slide right off. Cool to room temperature.

Begin the filling 20 minutes before you're ready to serve the tarts.

Spoon a heaping ¼ cup of filling into each tart shell. Don't worry about small cracks in the cups; the chocolate mixture is so thick it won't run out. If it does begin seeping out, refrigerate the filling for about 10 minutes before spooning it into any other cracked cups.

**Makes 24 tartlets**

## CHOCOLATE CREAM FILLING

| | |
|---|---|
| 12 OUNCES (1½ CUPS) SEMISWEET OR BITTERSWEET CHOCOLATE | 3 TABLESPOONS ORANGE LIQUEUR |
| | ½ CUP WHITE SUGAR |
| 6 LARGE EGGS | 1½ CUPS HEAVY CREAM |
| 3 TABLESPOONS STRONG COFFEE | 2 TEASPOONS VANILLA EXTRACT |

Melt the chocolate and set it aside to cool for at least 15 minutes. Then process or blend the eggs, coffee, and liqueur for about 30 seconds, until well mixed. Add the sugar and process for about 1 minute, until very frothy. Pour in the chocolate with the processor or blender running. When smooth, pour into a large bowl. Beat the cream until it holds soft peaks. Add the vanilla and beat until it holds stiff peaks. Stir one-quarter of the whipped cream into the chocolate mixture to lighten it, then fold in the remaining cream in 3 batches.

The tiny tartlet tins used in this recipe are the same as those used for Swedish Ginger Sand Tarts (see recipe, page 31) and come in several shapes, including diamonds, rectangles, pointed ovals, or hearts. They range from 2″ to 4″ across, are about ½″ deep, and have flat bottoms and angled, fluted sides. They can be found in most department-store housewares departments or mail-ordered (see "Mail Order Sources" chapter). For another lovely dessert inspired by those served at elegant French restaurants, bake tiny unfilled gingerbread shells for ten minutes at 350°F. Place a dollop of pastry or whipped cream in each baked shell and top with a large, perfect strawberry or a few raspberries, blackberries, or blueberries. Serve each person four tarts, one with each type of berry.

½ RECIPE GINGERBREAD TARTLET
SHELL DOUGH (PAGE 86)
6 OUNCES BLANCHED SLIVERED
ALMONDS (ABOUT 1 CUP)
6 TABLESPOONS UNSALTED BUTTER,

AT ROOM TEMPERATURE
6 TABLESPOONS CONFECTIONERS'
SUGAR
2 TEASPOONS VANILLA EXTRACT
1 LARGE EGG, PLUS 1 LARGE YOLK

Make the dough and refrigerate it for at least 2 hours, until cold. When ready to make the tarts, preheat the oven to 350°F. Toast the almonds on a baking sheet for 7 to 8 minutes, shaking the sheet occasionally, until the nuts are light brown all over. Leave the oven on when you remove the nuts. Coarsely grind the nuts in a food processor or nut grinder.

If you've used a nut grinder, turn the nuts out into a bowl at this point. If you're using the processor, continue with it. Process or beat in the butter, sugar, vanilla, egg, and yolk until you have a smooth paste. Set this frangipane mixture aside.

Grease 15 tartlet tins. Press an equal amount of the dough into each tin with your fingers, forming a shell ⅛″ thick. Spoon approximately 1¾ tablespoons frangipane into each.

Bake the tins on a baking sheet for 20 minutes, or until the shells are browned and the filling is puffed and lightly browned on top. Cool the tarts for 10 minutes in the tins, then carefully turn them out onto racks. Cool to room temperature.

**MAKES 15 TARTS**

Baked fruit dumplings are found throughout eastern Europe—Germany, Austria, Czechoslovakia—and in America. Betty Crocker's recipe, first given in 1904, was so popular it was printed on Gold Medal flour bags in the 1930s. My version uses a gingerbread dough. Though the dumplings look something like The Blob when baked, they're so good it doesn't matter. Serve with sweetened whipped cream, a custard sauce such as crème anglaise, or good store-bought praline sauce.

½ TEASPOON GROUND GINGER

½ TEASPOON GROUND CINNAMON

⅛ TEASPOON GROUND NUTMEG

⅛ TEASPOON GROUND CLOVES

⅛ TEASPOON SALT

¼ CUP PLUS 1 TABLESPOON
   UNSALTED BUTTER, CUT INTO
   SMALL PIECES

3 TABLESPOONS MOLASSES

5 TABLESPOONS BROWN SUGAR

1 LARGE EGG, SEPARATED

1¼ CUPS UNBLEACHED OR WHITE
   PRESIFTED ALL-PURPOSE FLOUR

2 TABLESPOONS RAISINS

2 VERY FIRM YELLOW DELICIOUS
   APPLES

Mix together the ginger, cinnamon, nutmeg, cloves, and salt and set aside.

Melt ¼ cup butter, remove from the heat, and scrape into a medium-size bowl. Beat in the molasses, then 3 tablespoons of the brown sugar. Stir in the spice mixture and egg yolk. When the mixture is smooth, stir in ¼ cup of the flour. Stir in the remaining flour in 4 batches just until completely moistened and smooth each time. Turn the dough out onto a piece of plastic or foil, wrap well, and refrigerate for 3 hours to 1 week.

When ready to make the dumplings, divide the dough in half, leaving one-half wrapped and refrigerated. Roll out the unwrapped dough on a floured board into a circle large enough to enclose one of the apples. Knead together the remaining 1 tablespoon butter, 2 tablespoons sugar, and the raisins. Peel one apple and core without cutting all the way through the bottom. Stuff with half the raisin mixture.

Brush the dough with the egg white. Place the apple in the center of the circle, then bring up the sides to enclose it. Pinch together the edges to seal. You can either overlap the dough or make decorative seams. Prepare the second dumpling the same way. If the dough becomes stiff at any point, work with slightly dampened hands.

Place the dumplings on a lightly greased baking sheet and refrigerate for 30 minutes to chill slightly. Preheat the oven to 450°F. Bake the apples for 10 minutes, then check them. Some of the dough will have drooped, and the dumplings resemble a derby hat at this point. That's fine unless part of the apple is left uncovered. In that case, push some dough up to cover it, using the flat side of a knife. Turn the oven down to 350° and bake for 20 minutes more, or until the apples are easily pierced with a skewer.

Cool the dumplings slightly, until warm but not hot. The inside of the dough will be slightly damp, but that's how it's supposed to be. Serve warm.

MAKES 2 DUMPLINGS

Cider pie is an old recipe from American Colonial times. Cider was boiled down to create a sweetener which tastes like superb honey with a strong apple flavor. You can still make cider "honey" today, as long as you have the raw unpasteurized, unfiltered kind usually sold only in apple season—fall and early winter. Store cider honey in a screwtop jar and use it instead of honey or as pancake syrup. I think you'll be so pleased you'll make the honey even when you have no intention of making this pie.

1 TABLESPOON UNSALTED BUTTER

¼ CUP CIDER "HONEY" (PAGE 93)

⅜ CUP WHITE SUGAR

2 TABLESPOONS LIGHT BROWN SUGAR

2 TABLESPOONS WATER

1 LARGE EGG, SEPARATED, PLUS 1 LARGE YOLK

¼ TEASPOON GROUND NUTMEG

¼ TEASPOON GROUND CINNAMON

2 TART APPLES (ABOUT 6 OUNCES EACH), PEELED, CORED, HALVED, AND THINLY SLICED

1 PREBAKED GINGER CRUMB PIECRUST (PAGE 93)

Preheat the oven to 350°F. Place the butter, cider honey, both sugars, and the water in a small saucepan. Begin simmering, stirring often, timing 5 minutes from when the sugars dissolve. Pour into a bowl and cool until just warm to the touch.

Whisk together the egg yolks, nutmeg, and cinnamon, then whisk into the cooled cider mixture. Beat the egg white until stiff and fold in.

Make an even layer of apple slices on the bottom of the crust. Gently pour in the cider custard without disturbing the apples. Bake the pie on a baking sheet for 40 minutes, until the custard is set. Cool on a rack and serve at room temperature.

**MAKES 8 SERVINGS**

**7 CUPS RAW UNPASTEURIZED, UNFILTERED CIDER**

In a medium-size saucepan boil the cider over high heat until half has evaporated. Keep brushing down the sides of the pan with a wet pastry brush to prevent sugar crystals from burning onto your pan.

Pour the 3½ cups of cider into a slightly smaller pan and boil over medium heat until half has evaporated. Keep brushing down the crystals on the sides.

Pour the 1¾ cups of cider into a very small saucepan. Boil over low heat until you have about ½ cup plus 2 tablespoons remaining. Don't let it get dark or it will harden as it cools. Pour into a glass jar, cool, and store.

**MAKES JUST OVER ½ CUP**

# GINGER CRUMB PIECRUST

I think every pie is better with this crust, but the cider and pecan custard pies are my two favorites. The formed but unbaked crust can be frozen in the pan, then turned out of the pan and stored, tightly wrapped in foil, for up to six months in the freezer. Replace the frozen crust in the pan and bake it for twelve to thirteen minutes rather than ten. The baked crust can be stored at room temperature for two days tightly wrapped in foil.

**1¾ CUPS GROUND GINGERSNAPS OR GINGER GRAHAM CRACKER CRUMBS (PAGE 25 OR 128)**

**¼ CUP UNSALTED BUTTER**

Preheat the oven to 350°F. Spread the crumbs in a 9″ pie pan.

Melt the butter, pour it into the pan, and stir with a fork until all the crumbs are moistened. Press out the crumbs with your fingers to form an even piecrust. Bake for 10 minutes, then cool completely in the pan on a wire rack.

**MAKES 1 PIECRUST**

This recipe evolved from a pecan pie that just wouldn't set. I was in a hurry and so annoyed that I turned the filling out, whisked in a couple more eggs, then tossed it back into the oven. The resulting custardy pie was so good that I've added the extra eggs ever since. It's a nice change from the usual, more syrupy pecan pie, and the ginger crust adds great flavor.

6 TABLESPOONS UNSALTED BUTTER, AT ROOM TEMPERATURE
1 CUP BROWN SUGAR
5 LARGE EGGS, LIGHTLY BEATEN
PINCH OF SALT
¾ CUP LIGHT CORN SYRUP

2 TABLESPOONS ORANGE LIQUEUR
1 TEASPOON VANILLA EXTRACT
1½ CUPS PECAN HALVES
1 PREBAKED GINGER CRUMB PIECRUST (PAGE 93)

Preheat the oven to 325°F. Beat together the butter and sugar, then beat in the eggs, salt, corn syrup, liqueur, and vanilla. Scatter the pecans evenly on the bottom of the piecrust. Carefully pour in the egg mixture without dislodging the nuts.

Set the pie pan on a baking sheet with 4 sides (in case the custard overflows) and bake for about 1 hour, until the filling is completely set and evenly puffed.

**MAKES 8 SERVINGS**

Brown Betty has always been one of my favorite desserts, and ginger-snaps make it even better. I love the contrast of the crunchy, sweet topping and the soft, tart fruit. If you substitute apples for the pears, use slightly tart ones such as Granny Smiths. Serve this hot, warm, or at room temperature, topped with vanilla ice cream or plain.

½ CUP WHITE SUGAR

2 TABLESPOONS MOLASSES

1 TABLESPOON ORANGE LIQUEUR

1 TABLESPOON VANILLA EXTRACT

4 CUPS PEELED RIPE PEARS (ABOUT
    4) CUT INTO ¾" CUBES

¾ CUP COARSE GINGERSNAP
    CRUMBS (PAGE 25)

1 TABLESPOON UNSALTED BUTTER,
    DICED

Stir together the sugar, molasses, liqueur, and vanilla extract in a bowl. Add the pear cubes and toss well to coat the pears completely. Let sit, covered with plastic wrap for about 1 hour at room temperature, tossing occasionally.

Preheat the oven to 350°F. Lightly butter a 1½-quart baking dish. Evenly cover the bottom with half the pear mixture. Top with half the ginger-snap crumbs, then half the butter. Repeat all three layers. Bake, covered, for 40 minutes. Uncover, turn the oven up to 400°, and bake for 10 minutes more to brown the top.

**MAKES 4 SERVINGS**

# BANANA FRITTERS

In the Caribbean, bananas and ginger are considered a perfect marriage. It's hardly surprising, since Jamaican ginger, the best in the world, turns normally bland foods into absolute delights. Caribbean banana fritters are especially good with pork or fish. They're also a delicious and easy dessert, but I like them best at breakfast, accompanied by fresh fruit, bacon, and coffee.

1 CUP UNBLEACHED OR WHITE PRESIFTED ALL-PURPOSE FLOUR

1 TEASPOON BAKING POWDER

¼ TEASPOON SALT

¼ CUP BROWN SUGAR

1 ¼ TEASPOONS GROUND GINGER

¾ TEASPOON GROUND CLOVES

1 ¼ TEASPOONS GROUND CINNAMON

¾ TEASPOON GROUND NUTMEG

½ CUP MILK

2 LARGE EGGS

TASTELESS VEGETABLE OIL (SUCH AS WESSON OR PEANUT)

3 RIPE BANANAS

CONFECTIONERS' SUGAR

Mix together the flour, baking powder, salt, sugar, ginger, cloves, cinnamon, and nutmeg in a bowl. Lightly beat the milk and eggs together to break up the yolks. Whisk this into the flour mixture just until smooth.

Pour the oil into a 9″ to 10″ skillet to a depth of ¾″ and heat over a medium flame to 375°F. Cut the peeled bananas into ½″ slices, then quarter the slices lengthwise. Fold them into the batter.

When the oil is hot, dip in the bowl of a soup spoon. Turn the heat to low. Using the oiled spoon, drop 5 or 6 spoonfuls of batter into the oil to form fritters about 2″ across. Cook, turning constantly, until dark golden brown all over. When they're browned, remove with a slotted spoon and drain on paper towels. Also remove any excess dough from the pan or it will blacken and ruin the oil. Make the rest of the fritters the same way, dipping the bowl of the soup spoon into the hot oil before each batch. Sprinkle with confectioners' sugar and serve immediately.

**MAKES 40 SMALL FRITTERS**

Chocolate truffles are usually rolled in cocoa, confectioners' sugar, or a mixture of both. However, given my great love of chocolate and ginger, a gingersnap coating seemed to be a natural. You can also add finely chopped candied ginger to the melted chocolate mixture. These are very rich, so don't expect to eat more than three or four. Store in the refrigerator, but remove to room temperature a couple of hours before you're planning to serve them.

¼ POUND CREAM CHEESE, AT ROOM
   TEMPERATURE
½ CUP UNSALTED BUTTER, AT ROOM
   TEMPERATURE
1 POUND BITTERSWEET CHOCOLATE,
   MELTED AND SLIGHTLY COOLED
¼ CUP CRÈME DE CACAO OR COFFEE

LIQUEUR
4 LARGE EGG YOLKS
2 TABLESPOONS UNSWEETENED
   COCOA POWDER, SIEVED TO RID OF
   LUMPS
1½ CUPS POWDERY GINGERSNAP
   CRUMBS (PAGE 25)

Beat together the cream cheese and butter until smooth. Beat in the chocolate, then the liqueur, yolks, and cocoa, until smooth. Refrigerate until the mixture is cold enough to roll into balls but not hard.

Place the crumbs in a small bowl. Using a melon baller or your hands, form the chocolate mixture into 1"-diameter balls. Roll the balls well in the crumbs.

Place the balls on a baking sheet or in a jelly-roll pan, not touching, and refrigerate until cold. When they're cold, reroll in the crumbs. Serve within a couple of hours or refrigerate.

**MAKES 60 TRUFFLES**

Let's face it, cream puffs are good, but they are a bit bland. Gingerbread cream puffs, on the other hand, are not only good, they're very good. My favorite filling for these are Cannoli or Chocolate Cream (see recipe, page 103 or 87), whipped cream, or ice cream.

| | |
|---|---|
| 1 CUP WATER | ⅛ TEASPOON SALT |
| ½ CUP UNSALTED BUTTER | ½ TEASPOON GROUND GINGER |
| 1 TABLESPOON MOLASSES | ½ TEASPOON GROUND CINNAMON |
| 1 CUP UNBLEACHED OR WHITE | ½ TEASPOON GROUND CLOVES |
|    PRESIFTED ALL-PURPOSE FLOUR | 4 LARGE EGGS |

In a medium-size saucepan bring the water, butter, and molasses to a boil over high heat. Mix together the flour, salt, ginger, cinnamon, and cloves. As soon as the liquid comes to a boil, turn the heat to low. Pour the flour mixture in all at once. Beat hard until the dough comes away from the sides of the pan and forms a ball in the center. Remove the pan from the heat and let sit for 5 minutes.

Preheat the oven to 450°F. Beat the eggs into the batter, 2 at a time, until completely incorporated. Drop 2 heaping tablespoons per cream puff about 2″ apart onto an ungreased baking sheet. You should have 10 puffs. Smooth out the tops with lightly dampened fingers. Bake for 15 minutes. Without opening the oven door, turn the heat down to 350°. Bake for 25 minutes more, or until the tops are golden and slightly browned.

Cool the puffs on the baking sheet set on a wire rack. When ready to serve, cut off the top of each puff and pull out any damp dough. Fill with your choice of cream, replace the tops, and serve immediately.

**MAKES 10 PUFFS**

VARIATION: If you want to delight children, make profiteroles: Drop a heaping teaspoon of dough for each puff rather than 2 tablespoons. Then bake them the same way, but only 10 to 15 minutes at 350°. Fill each with whipped or ice cream, then place as many as will fit into a tall parfait glass. Pour Caramel Sauce (page 57) or hot chocolate sauce over them and serve immediately.

# GINGERBREAD
## CHUNK ICE CREAM

This is such a simple recipe, but it's quite good. I prefer chocolate, vanilla, banana, butter pecan, or praline ice cream, but you can use any ice cream without a lot of other mix-ins already added. Premium ice creams, such as Häagen-Dazs, soften more quickly, so check the ice cream every ten minutes to see if it's soft enough to add the cookies.

1 PINT GOOD-QUALITY ICE CREAM
¾ CUP BASIC GINGERBREAD CAKE, ROLLED GINGERBREAD COOKIES, GINGERSNAPS, OR GINGER

BROWNIES (PAGE 52, 23, 25, OR 48), BROKEN INTO ½" SQUARES OR OTHER SMALL SHAPES

Let the ice cream sit outside the freezer in its container until the sides are very soft and the inside is still slightly hard. Turn out into a large bowl and mash with a spoon. Fold in the gingerbread pieces, being careful not to crush them. Pack into a plastic container and seal.

Freeze for at least 6 hours, until very cold. The ginger taste is almost negligible when the gingerbread is first added, but grows more intense with time. The ice cream should be eaten within 2 days, however, or the gingerbread dissolves.

**MAKES JUST OVER 1 PINT**

Potato doughnuts, once common throughout America, are now rarely found outside Idaho. You can't taste the potato; it just adds moisture to the dough. Homemade doughnuts are so delicious and easy that it's surprising more people don't make them. These must be eaten within two days, and preferably within one, or the ginger taste disappears.

4 CUPS UNBLEACHED OR WHITE
   PRESIFTED ALL-PURPOSE FLOUR
4 TEASPOONS BAKING POWDER
1 TEASPOON SALT
1 TEASPOON GROUND GINGER
½ TEASPOON GROUND CINNAMON
½ TEASPOON GROUND NUTMEG
¾ CUP PLUS 2 TABLESPOONS BROWN
   SUGAR

1 CUP MASHED POTATOES
2 TABLESPOONS UNSALTED BUTTER,
   DICED
6 TABLESPOONS MOLASSES
1 CUP HEAVY CREAM
2 LARGE EGGS, LIGHTLY BEATEN
TASTELESS VEGETABLE OIL (SUCH AS
   WESSON OR PEANUT)
CONFECTIONERS' SUGAR

Mix together well the flour, baking powder, salt, ginger, cinnamon, nutmeg, and brown sugar and set aside.

Heat the potatoes if they're not freshly made and place in a large bowl. Beat in the butter, then the molasses, cream, and eggs. Stir in the flour mixture just until smooth.

Pour the oil into a 9″ to 10″ skillet to a depth of 1″ and heat over a medium flame to 325°F. Turn out the dough and knead once or twice. Roll half out on a floured board until ½″ thick. Cut out 12 doughnuts with a 2½″ doughnut cutter. You can also use a 2½″ round cookie cutter, then cut the centers out manually. Add any dough scraps to the unused half.

Separate 4 doughnuts from their centers. Lightly pat each down until ¼″ thick. Slide the doughnuts and centers into the oil with a wide spatula. Cook, turning once, until golden brown all over. Remove with a slotted spoon and drain on paper towels. Don't eat while hot, since the insides continue to cook while the doughnuts are cooling. Fry the other 8 doughnuts and centers.

Roll out the remaining half of the dough. Cut into 13 doughnuts, then cut or pat out the excess into 3 extra "holes." Pat down, fry, and drain on paper towels. Cool the doughnuts to room temperature and sprinkle with confectioners' sugar. Store in a closed container.

**MAKES 25 DOUGHNUTS AND 28 "HOLES"**

In New York City's Little Italy, the true sign of a great bakery is terrific cannoli. While an authentic cannoli is a wonderful thing, a gingerbread cannoli is even better. For real ginger lovers there's also candied ginger in the filling. Experiment with other fillings if you prefer. Some bakers add chocolate chips to the ricotta mixture; others consider it heresy.

| | |
|---|---|
| 1 CUP UNBLEACHED OR WHITE PRESIFTED ALL-PURPOSE FLOUR | ¼ CUP BROWN SUGAR |
| 2¼ TEASPOONS GROUND GINGER | 4 TEASPOONS SWEET WHITE WINE |
| 2¼ TEASPOONS GROUND CINNAMON | 1 LARGE EGG PLUS 1 LARGE YOLK |
| 1¼ TEASPOONS GROUND CLOVES | TASTELESS VEGETABLE OIL |
| | 1 RECIPE FILLING (PAGE 103) |

In a large bowl mix together the flour, ginger, cinnamon, cloves, and sugar. Make a well in the center. Lightly beat together the wine, egg, and 1 tablespoon oil, then pour into the well. Using a fork, beginning with the area closest to the liquid, stir the flour into the center. When completely combined, beat briefly just until smooth. Wrap in plastic and let sit for 30 minutes at room temperature.

Pour oil into a 9″ to 10″ saucepan to a depth of 2″ and begin heating to 350°F. Oil 3 to 8 cannoli tubes. Roll the dough into 8 balls. On a lightly floured board, roll out each ball to a 5″ diameter. Wrap each around a cannoli tube and press gently to seal. Pull the dough gently, stretching it out to the length of the tube and thinning it slightly.

Deep-fry 3 or 4 cannoli at a time, turning once with tongs if necessary, about 3 minutes, until browned all over. Drain on a paper towel for about 1 minute. Then, holding one end of the tube with the tongs, push off the cannoli; use a sharp object if necessary to pry it off the metal. Cool to room temperature. The unfilled shells will keep for 2 days at room temperature in a tightly sealed container.

Just before serving, fill the shells with the cream, using a pastry bag with a wide round tip.

**MAKES 8 CANNOLI**

## CANNOLI FILLING

1 POUND WHOLE-MILK RICOTTA
   CHEESE

2 TEASPOONS VANILLA EXTRACT

½ CUP BROWN SUGAR

½ CUP FINELY CHOPPED CANDIED
   GINGER (OPTIONAL)

Blend or process the cheese, vanilla, and brown sugar together well. Pour into a bowl and fold in the ginger, if used. Press plastic wrap on top of the filling and refrigerate until ready to use.

Italy is famous for good reason for its elegant frozen desserts, including superb gelati and tortoni. While tortoni is usually made with amaretti —crisp, almond liqueur–flavored macaroons—ginger macaroons are also delicious. Tortoni can be frozen in any shape container. I prefer to make loaves, since they're easy to slice.

For a prettier presentation, freeze in greased fluted brioche molds or tartlet tins. Unmold them and serve on dessert plates painted with strawberry sauce. Top with a perfect strawberry where the knot of the brioche would be.

7/8 CUP COARSE GINGER MACAROON CRUMBS (PAGE 44)

3/4 CUP COARSELY GROUND BLANCHED ALMONDS

4 LARGE EGGS, SEPARATED

2 TABLESPOONS NUT LIQUEUR (SUCH AS FRANGELICO)

1/4 CUP WHITE SUGAR

1/4 CUP CONFECTIONERS' SUGAR

2 CUPS HEAVY CREAM

Preheat the oven to 350°F. Grease an adjustable loaf pan set to about 12¾" x 4½" or an 8"-x-3" round cake pan (not springform). Spread the crumbs and almonds on a baking sheet. Toast for about 7 minutes, stirring occasionally, until lightly browned. Pour into a bowl and cool completely. Remove 2 tablespoons and set aside.

Beat the yolks, liqueur, and both sugars together until smooth and pale yellow. In an electric mixer this will take 5 minutes at high speed. Fold in all but the 2 tablespoons of the cooled nut mixture.

Beat the cream until stiff and gently fold into the yolk mixture. Beat the egg whites until stiff, then fold them in. Pour the mixture into the pan and press plastic wrap onto the top. Freeze at least overnight or up to a month.

When ready to serve, soak a dish towel in hot water. Carefully peel off the plastic and place the tortoni pan upside down on a serving plate. Wring the towel out well, then drape it over the bottom and sides of the pan. As soon as possible, lift off the pan, leaving the tortoni on the plate. Serve immediately.

**MAKES 12 SERVINGS**

Ginger-flavored bread gives this old-fashioned dessert a whole new taste. It's even better if you serve it with your favorite hard sauce. Keep a resealable plastic bag in the freezer, marked "pudding," for bread just beginning to get stale. I often use two or three different kinds of bread in the pudding, and it's delicious.

¼ CUP UNSALTED BUTTER

¼ CUP WHITE SUGAR

2 MEDIUM APPLES AND/OR PEARS, PEELED, CORED, HALVED, AND THINLY SLICED

4 LARGE EGGS

3 CUPS MILK

1 TEASPOON VANILLA EXTRACT

½ CUP BROWN SUGAR

1 TABLESPOON GRATED LEMON OR ORANGE PEEL

5 CUPS ½"–1" CUBES OF STALE POTATO, WHOLE WHEAT, OR BANANA BREAD, OR BRIOCHES (PAGE 112, 114, 126, OR 118)

6 TABLESPOONS RAISINS

Melt the butter in a large skillet. Stir in the white sugar, then the apples, and toss well. Turn off the heat and let sit, uncovered, on the burner. Preheat the oven to 350°F. Butter a 2½-quart baking dish.

Whisk together the eggs, milk, vanilla, brown sugar, and lemon peel. Make an even layer of 2 cups bread cubes in the baking dish. Cover with the apples and raisins, then the remaining bread. Carefully pour in the milk mixture without disturbing the layers.

Set the filled baking dish in a shallow baking pan at least 2" wider in diameter. Place them in the oven. Pour very hot water into the shallow baking pan almost to the top. Make sure the sides of the baking dish and pan aren't touching each other at all. Bake for 1 hour, or until the center of the pudding is set.

**MAKES 8 TO 10 SERVINGS**

This intensely flavored topping is very versatile. It makes a good streusel mixture for coffee cakes and muffins. It's a perfect mix-in for ice cream, especially banana, or can be sprinkled on top of a sundae. Stir it into the batter of an unbaked cheesecake or sprinkle on top of any creamy dessert, such as mousse or pudding. I even snack on it. Stored in an airtight jar, it keeps for at least two months.

¼ CUP COARSELY GROUND PLUS ½ CUP ROUGHLY CHOPPED WALNUTS OR PECANS

¼ CUP VERY FINELY CHOPPED CANDIED GINGER

½ CUP COARSE GINGERSNAP OR GINGER MACAROON CRUMBS (PAGE 25 OR 44)

½ CUP UNBLEACHED, WHITE, OR WHOLE WHEAT FLOUR

½ CUP UNSALTED BUTTER, ROUGHLY CHOPPED

¼ CUP BROWN SUGAR

¼ CUP HONEY

Mix together the nuts, ginger, crumbs, and flour and set aside.

Melt the butter in a large skillet over very low heat. Stir in the sugar and honey just until evenly distributed in the pan. Preheat the oven to 250°F.

Stir the nut mixture into the skillet and cook for about 10 minutes, stirring often to break up, until crumbly. Remove the nut mixture with a slotted spoon and spread on a baking sheet. Bake for 40 minutes, breaking up the chunks on the baking sheet about every 10 minutes with the side of the slotted spoon.

Remove the baking sheet from the oven and, with a fork, mash and break up the ingredients until you have chunks roughly the size of peas. Let cool on the baking sheet, then drain well on paper towels.

**MAKES ABOUT 4 CUPS**

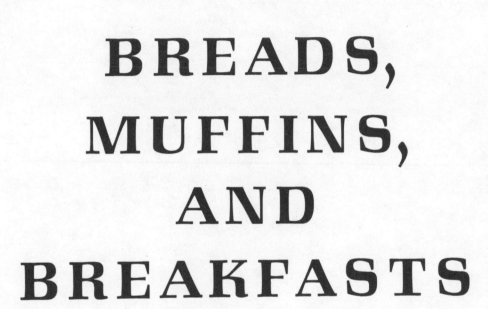

# BREADS, MUFFINS, AND BREAKFASTS

Today's gingerbreads are rarely breads; they've evolved into sweetened, somewhat dense cakes instead. Some New England restaurants still serve the cake with your meal, but that's becoming more and more rare. Even France's famous pain d'épices (spice bread) is closer to cake. The only true remaining spice breads, filled with dried pears and other preserved fruits, are made in Germany, France, Belgium, and Switzerland, usually only around Christmas.

Turning savory breads into ginger breads can be tricky. Temper the ginger and molasses with other spices, honey, and milk. If the taste is still slightly sharp after baking, spread on butter or honey and it will be fine. Toasted ginger bread is especially terrific in hot sandwiches like hamburgers or open-faced turkey, roast beef, or brisket with gravy. Yeast breads freeze well, so make as many loaves at one time as you have pans and patience for.

Once you've used potato in bread dough, you'll never bake without it again. It completely disappears, leaving your bread light and fluffy. The potato method described in the recipes below can be used in any yeast bread. All my yeast breads would be delicious with dried fruit folded in just before they're formed into loaves. Glaze fruit breads with a thin paste of confectioners' sugar and lemon juice.

If you're really interested in baking yeast breads, I strongly recommend the *Tassajara Bread Book* by Edward Espe Brown. Until I read it, my breads were always yeasty and I just never felt I knew what I was doing. Now I never make a bad loaf.

This was a good but ordinary loaf of white bread until it was enlivened with spices and molasses. It's extremely fluffy but still has substance. For years I've used a method for letting the dough rise which would make most authorities cry. Just before I start making the dough, I turn the oven to very low (200°F). Five minutes later I turn it off, never opening the door. Then I let the dough rise in the warm oven. The danger is that the heat will kill off the yeast or that the bread will rise too fast, but I find it always rises in textbook style. Use this bread as you would regular white bread. It's delicious for sandwiches, especially peanut butter and jelly or egg salad.

1 MEDIUM POTATO, PEELED, CUT INTO ½" CUBES

2¼ CUPS MILK, PLUS MORE IF NECESSARY

3½ TABLESPOONS HONEY

1 ¼-OZ. PACKAGE DRY YEAST

1½ TABLESPOONS MOLASSES

1 TABLESPOON SALT

1 TEASPOON GROUND GINGER

1 TEASPOON GROUND CINNAMON

½ TEASPOON GROUND CLOVES

½ TEASPOON GROUND NUTMEG

6 CUPS UNBLEACHED OR WHITE PRESIFTED ALL-PURPOSE FLOUR

¼ CUP UNSALTED BUTTER, MELTED AND COOLED SLIGHTLY

Place the potato and milk in a medium-size saucepan, turn heat to low, and simmer until the potato is tender. Drain the potato, reserving the milk. Pour ¼ cup of the milk into a small bowl, the rest into a large measuring cup. Mash the potato; if you have more than 1 cup, discard the excess. Cover the potato with foil and set aside.

When the ¼ cup of milk has cooled to about 110°F., stir in 1 tablespoon of the honey, and the yeast. Let sit for 5 minutes, until slightly frothy.

If you don't have 1¾ cups of milk in the measuring cup, add more. Pour the milk into a large bowl. Whisk in the mashed potato, molasses, remaining honey, salt, ginger, cinnamon, cloves, and nutmeg. Stir in the proofed yeast, scraping out the yeast bowl with a rubber spatula. Beat in 1½ cups of the flour until smooth. Cover the bowl with a towel and let the dough rise for 1 hour in a warm, draft-free place.

Beat the butter into the risen dough. Then beat in enough flour to make a soft but kneadable dough. Pour ½ cup of the remaining flour onto a board. Turn the dough out onto the board and knead for 10 minutes, adding just enough flour to prevent the dough from sticking. The dough should be soft but smooth and not sticky. Place in a lightly oiled bowl and turn to oil the dough on all sides. Cover with a towel and let rise for approximately 1 hour, until doubled in size.

Turn the dough out onto an unfloured board. Divide the dough in half, then knead each half several times until smooth. Roll each half into an 8″ long rope. Place each rope in a greased 8½″-x-4½″ loaf pan. Cover the pans loosely with towels and let rise for approximately 1 hour, until doubled in size.

Preheat the oven to 375°F. Bake the loaves for 40 minutes if in glass pans, 45 minutes if in metal. Turn the bread out of the pans, then bake the loaves on the oven racks for 10 minutes more, until browned all over.

**MAKES 2 LOAVES**

The ginger taste in this bread is very subtle but works beautifully. Use this as you would any everyday loaf of white or whole wheat bread. It's great for sandwiches, toast, or as a canapé base topped with cheese or meat.

| | |
|---|---|
| 3 CUPS UNBLEACHED OR WHITE PRESIFTED ALL-PURPOSE FLOUR | 5 TABLESPOONS MOLASSES |
| 3 CUPS WHOLE WHEAT FLOUR | 1 TABLESPOON SALT |
| 1 MEDIUM POTATO, PEELED, CUT INTO ½" CUBES | 1 TEASPOON GROUND GINGER |
| 2¼ CUPS MILK, PLUS MORE IF NECESSARY | 1 TEASPOON GROUND CINNAMON |
| | ¾ TEASPOON GROUND CLOVES |
| | ½ TEASPOON GROUND NUTMEG |
| 2 TABLESPOONS HONEY | ½ TEASPOON GROUND MACE |
| 1 PACKAGE DRY YEAST | ¼ CUP UNSALTED BUTTER, MELTED AND SLIGHTLY COOLED |

Mix together the flours and set aside. Place the potato and milk in a medium-size saucepan, turn heat to low, and simmer until the potato is tender. Drain the potato, reserving the milk. Pour ¼ cup of the milk into a small bowl, the rest into a large measuring cup. Mash the potato; if you have more than 1 cup, discard it. Cover the potato with foil and set aside.

When the ¼ cup of milk has cooled to about 110°F., stir in the honey and the yeast. Let sit for 5 minutes until slightly frothy.

If you don't have 1¾ cups of milk in the measuring cup, add more. Pour the milk into a large bowl. Whisk in the potato, molasses, salt, ginger, cinnamon, cloves, nutmeg, and mace. Stir in the proofed yeast, scraping out the yeast bowl with a rubber spatula. Beat in 1½ cups of the combined flours until smooth. Cover the bowl with a towel and let the dough rise for 1 hour in a warm, draft-free place.

Stir the butter into the risen dough, then beat in enough flour to make a soft but kneadable dough. Pour ½ cup of the remaining flour onto a board. Turn the dough out onto the board and knead for 10 minutes, adding just enough flour to prevent the dough from sticking. The dough should be soft but smooth and not sticky. Place in a lightly oiled bowl, turning to oil the dough on all sides. Cover with a towel and let rise for approximately 1 hour, until doubled in size.

Turn the dough out onto an unfloured board. Divide the dough in half, then knead each half several times until smooth. Roll each into an 8″-long rope. Place each rope in a greased 8½″-x-4½″ loaf pan. Cover the pans loosely with towels and let rise for approximately 1 hour, until doubled in size.

Preheat the oven to 375°F. Bake the loaves for 40 minutes if in glass pans, 45 minutes if in metal. Turn the bread out of the pans, then bake the loaves on the oven racks for another 10 minutes, until browned all over.

**MAKES 2 LOAVES**

Very gingery when it first comes out of the oven, this corn bread is much milder at room temperature. Corn bread, especially this one, makes great stuffing, so try it out in chicken (see recipe, page 146) or turkey. For southwestern-style corn bread, add minced jalapeños, crumbled cooked sausage, and grated sharp cheese to the batter. Serve this alongside any spicy meat or poultry, especially Cajun, Latin American, southwestern, or Indian food. If you prefer, you can bake this in muffin tins or corn-stick pans at 400°F., until a skewer comes out clean. When turning the bread out of the pan, a ten-inch wire cake rack is just the right size.

| | |
|---|---|
| 1½ CUPS YELLOW CORNMEAL | 1¼ CUPS MILK |
| 1 CUP UNBLEACHED OR WHITE PRESIFTED ALL-PURPOSE FLOUR | 3 TABLESPOONS HONEY |
| 2 TEASPOONS SALT | ¾ TEASPOON GROUND GINGER |
| 1 TEASPOON PEPPER | ½ TEASPOON GROUND CLOVES |
| 1¼ TABLESPOONS BAKING POWDER | ¼ TEASPOON GROUND NUTMEG |
| 2 LARGE EGGS | 1½ TABLESPOONS UNSALTED BUTTER |

Preheat the oven to 400°F. Mix together the cornmeal, flour, salt, pepper, and baking powder in a large bowl.

Lightly beat together the eggs, milk, honey, ginger, cloves, and nutmeg, then stir into the flour mixture just until combined.

Melt the butter in a 9″ ovenproof skillet, preferably cast-iron. Tilt the pan to coat the bottom and sides completely. Pour in the batter and place in the oven. Bake for 30 minutes, or until a skewer in the center comes out clean.

Remove the pan from the oven. Run a knife around the sides. Place a wire rack over the pan and turn the pan and rack over at the same time. The bread will fall right out. Cool to room temperature.

**MAKES 10 TO 12 SERVINGS**

Quick breads don't need to rise before baking, since baking powder or soda replaces the yeast. Delicious hot and fresh, this bread begins losing flavor in a day or two, until the onions can't be distinguished. I usually use this as the base for canapés such as cheese and sun-dried tomato croutes (see recipe, page 157). You can also top small triangles of toasted, fried, or plain bread with chicken and chutney, steak tartare, any kind of creamy cheese, or rumaki. Please note that this sophisticated bread is an adult-pleaser, not a child's favorite.

2 CUPS WHOLE WHEAT FLOUR

2½ CUPS UNBLEACHED OR WHITE
   PRESIFTED ALL-PURPOSE FLOUR

¼ CUP BROWN SUGAR

2 CUPS MILK

¼ CUP UNSALTED BUTTER, MELTED
   AND COOLED

3 LARGE EGGS

2 TABLESPOONS MOLASSES

1 TEASPOON GROUND GINGER

1 TEASPOON GROUND CINNAMON

1 TEASPOON GROUND CLOVES

2 TEASPOONS SALT

4 TEASPOONS BAKING POWDER

¾ CUP COARSELY CHOPPED WALNUTS

½ CUP COARSELY CHOPPED ONION

Preheat the oven to 325°F. Grease two 8½"-x-4½" loaf pans. Mix together the flours and sugar in a large bowl.

In a separate bowl whisk together the milk, butter, eggs, molasses, ginger, cinnamon, cloves, salt, and baking powder, then stir into the flour. Gently fold in the walnuts and onion. Don't overmix.

Spoon the batter into the loaf pans and smooth out the tops with dampened hands. Slash each loaf once lengthwise. Bake for about 1½ hours, until a skewer inserted in the center of the loaves comes out clean. Immediately turn the loaves out of the pans onto a rack to cool.

**MAKES 2 LOAVES**

These spice-and-molasses-flavored brioches would horrify a French-man dedicated to authenticity, but who cares? They're very fluffy and tasty. Perfect hot or at room temperature for breakfast, they can also be served with dinner or sliced and made into French Toast (see recipe, page 137). If you like your breads as sweet as Hawaiian or Portuguese sweet bread, add one or two more tablespoons of honey. I prefer to spread dark honey on the baked brioche. Brioches freeze very well and are easily reheated in a microwave.

1 SMALL POTATO, PEELED, CUT INTO
  ½" CUBES
1 CUP MILK
¼ CUP HONEY
4½ TEASPOONS (ALMOST 2 ¼-OZ.
  PACKAGES) DRY YEAST
2 TABLESPOONS MOLASSES
6 TABLESPOONS UNSALTED BUTTER,
  MELTED AND SLIGHTLY COOLED
1 TEASPOON SALT

1 ½ TEASPOONS GROUND GINGER
1 ½ TEASPOONS GROUND CINNAMON
¼ TEASPOON GROUND CLOVES
¼ TEASPOON GROUND NUTMEG
3 CUPS UNBLEACHED OR WHITE
  PRESIFTED ALL-PURPOSE FLOUR
4 LARGE EGGS
1 LARGE EGG YOLK LIGHTLY BEATEN
  WITH 1 TABLESPOON MILK

Place the potato and milk in a medium-size saucepan, turn heat to low, and simmer until the potato is tender. Drain the potato, reserving the milk. Pour the milk into a small bowl and set aside. Mash the potato; if you have more than ½ cup, discard it. Place the potato into a large bowl, cover with foil, and set aside.

When the milk has cooled to about 110°F., stir in 1 tablespoon of the honey, and the yeast. Let sit for 5 minutes, until slightly frothy.

Whisk the molasses, remaining honey, butter, salt, ginger, cinnamon, cloves, and nutmeg into the potato. Stir in the proofed yeast, scraping out the yeast bowl with a rubber spatula. Beat in 1 cup of the flour until smooth. Cover with a towel and let rise for about 1 hour in a warm, draft-free place until doubled.

Beat the eggs into the risen dough, then enough flour to make the dough kneadable. Turn out onto a floured board. Knead for 5 minutes, until very smooth, adding just enough flour to make a very soft and slightly damp dough. Place in an oiled bowl and turn the dough to oil on all sides. Let rise, covered with a towel, for about 1½ hours, until doubled.

Grease 12 brioche molds, large tartlet tins, or muffin cups. Turn the dough out onto a lightly floured board. Working with damp hands, divide into 12 pieces. Keep your hands damp as you work, since the dough is slightly sticky. Divide one of the twelfths into 2 pieces—one of which is one-sixth of the dough, the other five-sixths. Roll and pat the larger piece into a ball and place, seam side down, in a mold, tin, or cup. Poke a ¼″ deep hole in the center with a damp finger. Form the smaller piece into a teardrop and place, point side down, in the hole. Make the rest of the brioches the same way. Place the brioche molds on a baking sheet.

Let rise for approximately 45 minutes, until the body of the brioche (not the ball on top) is even with the top of the mold. Preheat the oven to 400°F.

Lightly brush the brioches with the yolk mixture. Bake for 20 minutes, or until browned. Turn out and cool on a wire rack.

**MAKES 12 BRIOCHES**

Slightly harsh when eaten plain, these are delicious when buttered. The secret to good biscuits is not to handle them too much or they become rubbery. I used the top of a quarter-cup dry measure to cut out the biscuits.

If you split the biscuits and top each half with a spoonful of whipped cream and a few fresh berries, you have old-fashioned shortcake. Serve the shortcake with assorted rolls, sliced melon, sliced ham or bacon, and baked eggs for a lovely Sunday company breakfast requiring very little last-minute work.

2 CUPS UNBLEACHED OR WHITE PRESIFTED ALL-PURPOSE FLOUR

6 TABLESPOONS UNSALTED BUTTER

1 CUP BUTTERMILK

2 TABLESPOONS HONEY

½ TEASPOON GROUND GINGER

½ TEASPOON GROUND CINNAMON

½ TEASPOON GROUND CLOVES

½ TEASPOON GROUND NUTMEG

¼ TEASPOON SALT

1 TABLESPOON BAKING POWDER

Place the flour in a large bowl. Dice 4 tablespoons of the butter and cut into the flour until you have particles the size of grains of rice. Make a well in the center.

In a separate bowl whisk together the buttermilk, honey, ginger, cinnamon, cloves, nutmeg, salt, and baking powder. Pour into the well in the flour. Stir lightly with a fork just until the flour is completely moistened.

Preheat the oven to 450°F. Turn the dough out onto a lightly floured board. Knead 4 or 5 times until smooth. Pat out ¼" thick. Cut into twenty 2" rounds.

Melt the remaining butter. Brush half the rounds with butter, then top with the remaining rounds. Place on an ungreased baking sheet and brush the tops with butter. Bake for 12 to 14 minutes, until lightly browned.

**MAKES 10 BISCUITS**

Scones are either baked in the oven or cooked on a griddle. Each method has its advantages: When oven-baked, they're less sweet, fluffier, and more delicate tasting. When they're cooked on the griddle, the outside has a nice toasty flavor and look. I prefer them oven-baked, since I split the cooked scones—with a fork, never a knife—and toast the inside anyway. Serve with butter and jam, jelly, or preserves.

| | |
|---|---|
| ¼ CUP UNSALTED BUTTER, MELTED | ¼ TEASPOON GROUND CLOVES |
| ½ CUP BROWN SUGAR | ½ TEASPOON SALT |
| ½ CUP SOUR CREAM | 1 ½ TEASPOONS BAKING SODA |
| 1 TEASPOON GROUND GINGER | 2 CUPS UNBLEACHED OR WHITE |
| 1 TEASPOON GROUND CINNAMON | PRESIFTED ALL-PURPOSE FLOUR |
| ¼ TEASPOON GROUND NUTMEG | |

Beat the butter and sugar together until smooth. Beat in the sour cream, then the ginger, cinnamon, nutmeg, cloves, salt, and baking soda. Stir in the flour until the mixture forms a soft dough.

Turn the dough out onto a lightly floured board. Pat out half into a 6½″ circle about ⅜″ thick. Cut the circle into 6 wedges. Repeat with the remaining dough.

Oven method: Bake the wedges on an ungreased baking sheet in a pre-heated 400°F. oven for 15 minutes.

Griddle method: Bake for 2 to 3 minutes on a floured or nonstick griddle heated on a low flame until the dough is opaque halfway up the sides of the wedges and lightly browned on the bottom. Turn with a spatula and brown the second side. Let sit for 5 minutes before serving, since the inside continues to cook.

**MAKES 12 SCONES**

Though often relegated to baby food, these are much too good to stop eating just because you have all your teeth. *Zwieback* means "twice baked," because you simply take a small bread, slice it, and bake the slices until they're dry. These are great for an upset stomach when you want something with a little more flavor than plain toast.

1 MEDIUM POTATO, PEELED, CUT
   INTO ½" CUBES
2¼ CUPS MILK, PLUS MORE IF
   NECESSARY
5 TABLESPOONS HONEY
1 PACKAGE DRY YEAST
3 TABLESPOONS MOLASSES
1 TABLESPOON SALT

1¼ TEASPOONS GROUND GINGER
1¼ TEASPOONS GROUND CINNAMON
½ TEASPOON GROUND CLOVES
½ TEASPOON GROUND NUTMEG
6 CUPS UNBLEACHED OR WHITE
   PRESIFTED ALL-PURPOSE FLOUR
¼ CUP UNSALTED BUTTER, MELTED
   AND SLIGHTLY COOLED

Place the potato and milk in a medium-size saucepan, turn heat to low, and simmer until the potato is tender. Drain the potato, reserving the milk. Pour ¼ cup of the milk into a small bowl, the rest into a large measuring cup. Mash the potato; if you have more than 1 cup, discard it. Cover the potato with foil and set aside.

When the ¼ cup of milk has cooled to about 110°F., stir in 1 tablespoon of the honey, and the yeast. Let sit for 5 minutes, until slightly frothy.

If you don't have 1¾ cups of milk in the measuring cup, add more. Pour the milk into a large bowl. Whisk in the mashed potato, molasses, remaining honey, salt, ginger, cinnamon, cloves, and nutmeg. Stir in the proofed yeast, scraping out the yeast bowl with a rubber spatula. Beat in 1½ cups of the flour until smooth. Cover the bowl with a towel and let the dough rise for 1 hour in a warm, draft-free place.

Beat the butter into the risen dough, then add enough flour to make a soft but kneadable dough. Pour ½ cup of the remaining flour onto a board. Turn the dough out onto the board and knead for 10 minutes, adding just enough flour to prevent the dough from sticking. The dough should be soft but smooth and not sticky. Place in a lightly oiled bowl and turn the dough to oil it on all sides. Cover with a towel and let rise for approximately 1 hour, until doubled in size.

Turn the dough out onto an unfloured board. Divide it into quarters. Knead each piece once or twice until smooth. Gently roll each into an 8″ rope. Place each rope in a greased 8½″-x-4½″ loaf pan. Pull and stretch gently to fill the bottom of the pans evenly and completely. Cover the loaves with towels and let rise for approximately 1 hour, until doubled in size.

Preheat the oven to 375°F. Bake the loaves for 40 minutes if in glass pans, 45 minutes if in metal. Turn the bread out of the pans and cool completely on wire racks.

Cut each loaf into slices ½″ to ¾″ thick. Place the slices, one cut side down, on an ungreased baking sheet. Put into a cold oven, then turn the heat to 250°. Bake for 2 to 3 hours, until completely dried out.

**MAKES 48 SLICES**

This is the gingerbread version of cinnamon rolls. They're made with a sweetened bread dough filled with brown sugar, nuts, and raisins, so they're appropriate for either breakfast or a snack. You can use white flour rather than whole wheat if you prefer. Whole wheat makes a stronger-tasting dough, but both are good.

3 CUPS WHOLE WHEAT FLOUR

2 CUPS UNBLEACHED OR WHITE PRESIFTED ALL-PURPOSE FLOUR

1 SMALL POTATO, PEELED, CUT INTO ½" CUBES

2 CUPS MILK, PLUS MORE IF NECESSARY

3 TABLESPOONS LIGHT CORN SYRUP

1 PACKAGE DRY YEAST

2 TABLESPOONS MOLASSES

1 TABLESPOON SALT

1½ TEASPOONS GROUND GINGER

1 TEASPOON GROUND CINNAMON

½ TEASPOON GROUND CLOVES

½ TEASPOON GROUND NUTMEG

6 TABLESPOONS UNSALTED BUTTER, MELTED AND SLIGHTLY COOLED

1 LARGE EGG, PLUS 1 LARGE WHITE

½ CUP BROWN SUGAR

2 CUPS COARSELY CHOPPED WALNUTS

1 CUP RAISINS

Mix together both flours and set aside. Place the potato and milk in a medium-size saucepan, turn heat to low, and simmer until the potato is tender. Drain the potato, reserving the milk. Pour ¼ cup of the milk into a small bowl, the rest into a measuring cup. Mash the potato; if you have more than 1 cup, discard it. Cover the potato with foil and set aside.

When the ¼ cup of milk has cooled to about 110°F., stir in 1 tablespoon of the corn syrup, and the yeast. Let sit 5 minutes, until slightly frothy.

If you don't have 1¼ cups milk in the measuring cup, add more. Pour the milk into a large bowl. Whisk in the potato, molasses, remaining corn syrup, salt, ginger, cinnamon, cloves, and nutmeg. Stir in the proofed yeast, scraping out the yeast bowl with a rubber spatula. Beat in 1½ cups of the combined flours until smooth. Cover the bowl with a towel and let the dough rise for 1 hour in a warm, draft-free place.

Beat 4 tablespoons of the butter into the risen dough, then the egg and egg white. Beat in 2½ cups more flour to make a soft but kneadable dough. Spread the remaining 1 cup flour on a board. Turn the dough out onto the board and knead 10 minutes, until still soft but smooth and not sticky. Place in a lightly oiled bowl and turn the dough on all sides. Cover with a towel and let rise for approximately 1 hour, until doubled in size.

Turn the dough out onto a lightly floured board. Pat out into a large rectangle. Then, with as few strokes as possible, roll it out until it's 12″ by 18″. Brush with the remaining 2 tablespoons butter. Sprinkle evenly with the brown sugar, nuts, and raisins.

Roll the dough up, jelly-roll fashion, beginning with one long side. It will be an 18″ log. Carefully cut it into nine 2″-wide slices. Lay the slices on a baking sheet, 2″ apart, and let rise for 45 to 60 minutes, until doubled.

Preheat the oven to 375°F. Bake the rolls for 30 minutes, until browned all over. It's all right if they expand to touch each other during baking, since they can easily be pulled apart.

**MAKES 9 ROLLS**

Like the Banana-Nut Cupcakes (see recipe, page 80), these muffins are even better when made with exotic bananas. Mary Sue Milliken, of the highly esteemed City Restaurant in Los Angeles, likes to serve banana bread with fruit salad at lunch. I agree, and I also think it is perfect alongside a soup and salad supper. In the Virgin Islands, banana bread accompanied by a cup of yogurt is considered a perfect breakfast.

1½ CUPS (APPROXIMATELY 3) VERY RIPE BANANAS

½ CUP DARK BROWN SUGAR

6 TABLESPOONS UNSALTED BUTTER, MELTED

2 LARGE EGGS

1 TEASPOON BAKING SODA

½ TEASPOON SALT

1 TEASPOON GROUND CINNAMON

¼ TEASPOON GROUND ALLSPICE

¼ TEASPOON GROUND NUTMEG

2 TABLESPOONS FRESH GINGER, MINCED VERY FINE OR MASHED THROUGH A GARLIC PRESS

1½ CUPS UNBLEACHED OR WHITE PRESIFTED ALL-PURPOSE FLOUR

Preheat the oven to 350°F. for bread, 400°F. for muffins. (Grease a metal 8½"-x-4½" loaf pan or 10 muffin cups.) Process or mash and beat the banana until smooth. Then process or beat in the remaining ingredients except the flour. When the mixture is completely smooth, fold in the flour just until completely moistened.

To make bread: Spoon the mixture into the pan. Bake for 60 to 70 minutes, until a skewer inserted into the middle of the loaf comes out clean. Cool the pan on a wire rack for 30 minutes, then turn the loaf out onto the rack and cool completely.

To make muffins: Spoon the batter into the muffin cups and bake for 20 minutes at 400°F. Let cool for 15 minutes, then turn out onto a wire rack.

**MAKES 1 LOAF OR 10 MUFFINS**

This recipe is adapted from the *Tassajara Bread Book*. I sometimes make muffins in brioche molds or tartlet tins, so they look like tiny fluted tartlets. It's nice to get some other use out of those molds. These muffins are quite small, just a few bites, so you can satisfy your craving without going overboard.

| | |
|---|---|
| 1 CUP WHOLE WHEAT FLOUR | 1 ¼ CUPS MILK |
| 1 CUP UNPROCESSED BRAN | 1 TEASPOON GROUND GINGER |
| 6 TABLESPOONS MOLASSES | 1 TEASPOON GROUND CINNAMON |
| ¼ CUP UNSALTED BUTTER, MELTED | ½ TEASPOON GROUND NUTMEG |
| AND COOLED | ½ TEASPOON SALT |
| 1 LARGE EGG, LIGHTLY BEATEN | 2 TEASPOONS BAKING POWDER |

Preheat the oven to 400°F. Grease 12 muffin tins (or tartlet tins). Mix the flour and bran together well and set aside.

In a separate bowl stir the molasses into the butter, then stir in the egg, milk, ginger, cinnamon, nutmeg, salt, and baking powder. Fold in the flour mixture, half at a time, just until moistened. Don't overmix or the muffins will be rubbery.

Spoon the batter into the muffin cups. Bake for about 20 minutes, until a skewer inserted into the center of a muffin comes out clean. Run a sharp knife around the sides of the muffins and turn out onto a wire rack to cool.

**MAKES 12 SMALL MUFFINS**

The problem with store-bought graham crackers—aside from the fact that they aren't gingerbread-flavored—is that they're sometimes stale. If you make your own, you never have to worry about freshness. These are very thin and crispy, and I think they're better than the store-bought variety. I always make extra crackers, since the crumbs make great cheesecake and pie crusts and other desserts. Spread them with cream cheese and serve alongside hot soup, or grab a few crackers as you're rushing out the door in the morning. Make more than you think you'll need, since they disappear fast.

1 TEASPOON BAKING POWDER

½ TEASPOON BAKING SODA

½ TEASPOON SALT

1 TEASPOON GROUND GINGER

1 TEASPOON GROUND CLOVES

½ TEASPOON GROUND CINNAMON

1 CUP WHOLE WHEAT OR GRAHAM
   FLOUR

1 CUP UNBLEACHED OR WHITE
   PRESIFTED ALL-PURPOSE FLOUR

½ CUP UNSALTED BUTTER

¼ CUP HONEY

2 TABLESPOONS MOLASSES

½ CUP DARK BROWN SUGAR

Mix together the baking powder and soda, salt, ginger, cloves, cinnamon, and both flours and set aside.

In a medium-size saucepan melt the butter over low heat, then stir in the honey, molasses, and sugar. Add the flour mixture and beat well.

Turn the dough out onto a sheet of plastic wrap and pat into a rectangle. Wrap well and refrigerate for 4 hours to 2 days.

Remove the dough from the refrigerator and let sit at room temperature for 15 minutes to make it slightly more workable. Preheat the oven to 350°F.

Roll out one-quarter of the dough ⅛″ thick on a floured board. Using a pastry cutter or a ruler and sharp knife, cut into 10 rectangles. Separate the rectangles, then roll each out until approximately 4½″ by 3″. Prick with the tines of a fork in an even pattern until each has 5 rows of 8 tiny holes.

Using a wide spatula, carefully transfer the crackers to an ungreased baking sheet, placing them ½″ apart. Bake for 12 minutes only. While they're baking, make the rest of the crackers. As soon as you've removed the baking sheet from the oven, transfer the crackers to a rack with the spatula and cool completely.

**MAKES 40 CRACKERS**

While everyday pancakes are good, these are enough to make even the most devoted night person smile. Top them with New England maple syrup or Cider "Honey" (see recipe, page 93). Or spread them with your best homemade preserves. For a Caribbean flavor, stir coconut into the batter and replace the milk with fresh, canned, or thawed frozen unsweetened coconut milk or cream. If you use the coconut milk instead of regular milk and omit the butter, these can be served to children (or adults) who are allergic to milk.

¾ CUP MILK

1 LARGE EGG, PLUS 1 LARGE WHITE

2 TABLESPOONS MOLASSES

½ TEASPOON GROUND GINGER

¼ TEASPOON GROUND NUTMEG

¼ TEASPOON GROUND CLOVES

PINCH OF SALT

1 TEASPOON BAKING POWDER

1 CUP UNBLEACHED OR WHITE
   PRESIFTED ALL-PURPOSE FLOUR

2 TABLESPOONS UNSALTED BUTTER,
   MELTED AND SLIGHTLY COOLED

Whisk together the milk, egg, egg white, molasses, ginger, nutmeg, cloves, salt, and baking powder. Fold in the flour just until completely moistened, then the butter. Refrigerate overnight.

Heat a seasoned or a Teflon griddle, or a lightly greased griddle or large skillet. Using half the batter, drop 2 tablespoons of batter, one atop the other, for each of 4 pancakes. As soon as the pancake rises slightly and the top surface bubbles around the edges and looks as though it won't run, flip it over with a spatula. Cook only a minute or two on the other side, until lightly browned. Repeat with the remaining batter. Serve on heated plates.

**MAKES 8 PANCAKES**

I've seen people in southern restaurants accompany their main dish with corn pancakes or fritters, hush puppies (made with cornmeal), *and* fresh corn on the cob. Ginger and corn is an inspired combination. The spiciness and starchy sweetness complement each other beautifully. Serve these alongside any pork dish—especially barbecue, pork chops, or ham—or any kind of chicken.

2 LARGE EGGS, PLUS 2 LARGE WHITES

½ CUP BUTTERMILK

½ TEASPOON SALT

¼ TEASPOON PEPPER

1 TEASPOON GROUND GINGER

1 TEASPOON GROUND CINNAMON

½ TEASPOON GROUND NUTMEG

¼ TEASPOON GROUND CARDAMOM

3 TABLESPOONS HONEY

½ CUP UNBLEACHED OR WHITE PRESIFTED ALL-PURPOSE FLOUR

¼ CUP WHITE OR YELLOW CORNMEAL

2 CUPS COOKED CORN KERNELS (FROM 3 LARGE OR 4 MEDIUM EARS)

¼ CUP FINELY CHOPPED ONION

4–6 TABLESPOONS UNSALTED BUTTER, PREFERABLY CLARIFIED

Whisk together the eggs, egg whites, buttermilk, salt, pepper, ginger, cinnamon, nutmeg, cardamom, and honey. Fold in the flour and cornmeal just until moistened. Fold in the corn and onion.

In a 10″ skillet melt 2 tablespoons of the butter over low heat. Drop in 5 pancakes, 2 tablespoons of batter each. Fry for approximately 2 minutes, until set around the sides and golden on the bottom. Turn them over and fry the other side for about 1 minute, until set. Drain on paper towels. Fry the remaining pancakes, adding more butter as necessary to prevent sticking.

**MAKES TWENTY-SIX 3″ PANCAKES**

I came back with three vivid memories from my first trip to The Netherlands, a country I love to visit over and over again: the fantastic miniature city of Madurodam; farm—not the usual factory—Gouda, one of the finest cheeses in the world; and the apple pancakes served at the Amsterdam Hilton. These are closer to thin, crisp Yorkshire pudding than American-style fluffy pancakes. Traditionally, they're called cobbler's pancakes, but I don't know why. Since the Dutch were major spice importers from Asia, perhaps they'll forgive my adding ginger to an already almost-perfect dish.

⅜ CUP MILK

1 LARGE EGG

½ TABLESPOON MOLASSES

⅛ TEASPOON SALT

¼ TEASPOON BAKING POWDER

¼ TEASPOON GROUND GINGER

¼ TEASPOON GROUND CINNAMON

¼ TEASPOON GROUND CLOVES

⅛ TEASPOON GROUND CARDAMOM

½ CUP UNBLEACHED OR WHITE PRESIFTED ALL-PURPOSE FLOUR

¼ CUP UNSALTED BUTTER

2 TABLESPOONS BROWN SUGAR

1 TART APPLE (SUCH AS GRANNY SMITH), PEELED, CORED, HALVED, AND CUT INTO ¼"-THICK SLICES

Whisk together the milk, egg, molasses, salt, baking powder, ginger, cinnamon, cloves, and cardamom. Whisk in the flour until the mixture is lump-free. Pour into a large measuring cup with a spout.

Melt 2 tablespoons of the butter in an 8″ skillet over low heat. Stir in the brown sugar 1 to 2 seconds to mix well. Add the apple slices and sauté them for 3 to 4 minutes. Turn after the first 2 minutes, and stir to distribute them evenly in the pan.

Immediately after turning the apples, melt the remaining 2 tablespoons butter in another 8″ skillet over high heat. Pour in the batter and cook until the bottom is completely set. Quickly turn the pan over so that the pancake falls, uncooked side down, into the apple skillet. Cook for 3 minutes more, until the bottom is set. Turn out, sugar side up, onto a large plate. Serve hot.

**MAKES 2 SERVINGS**

If you like dessert waffles, top these with praline, banana, or vanilla ice cream, pour on Caramel Sauce (see recipe, page 57), and sprinkle with grated bittersweet chocolate. Feel free to add items to the waffle batter such as pecans, walnuts, hazelnuts, blueberries, or chocolate chunks. If you prefer brunch waffles (these are a bit too sweet for breakfast), serve with maple syrup or Cider "Honey" (see recipe, page 93) on the side. You can also top them with fresh fruit and whipped cream or simply sprinkle with confectioners' sugar and cinnamon.

3 LARGE EGGS, SEPARATED, PLUS 2 LARGE WHITES

¼ CUP BUTTER, MELTED AND SLIGHTLY COOLED

¾ CUP BROWN SUGAR

1 CUP BUTTERMILK

¼ CUP MOLASSES

4 TEASPOONS GRATED OR FINELY CHOPPED ORANGE RIND

1 TABLESPOON GRATED FRESH GINGER

1 TEASPOON GROUND CINNAMON

½ TEASPOON GROUND CLOVES

¼ TEASPOON GROUND NUTMEG

½ TEASPOON SALT

1 TEASPOON BAKING SODA

2 TEASPOONS BAKING POWDER

2 CUPS UNBLEACHED OR WHITE PRESIFTED ALL-PURPOSE FLOUR

Beat the egg yolks until lemon-colored and thick. Beat in the butter and sugar, then the buttermilk, molasses, orange rind, ginger, cinnamon, cloves, nutmeg, salt, baking soda and baking powder.

Stir in the flour just until moistened. Beat the 5 egg whites until stiff and fold into the batter. Cook in a waffle iron according to the manufacturer's instructions.

MAKES TEN 6"-x-5" WAFFLES

Like the usual unspiced blintzes, these are equally good with strawberries, cheese, or sautéed apples or pears. The pancakes can also be used in both savory and sweet recipes calling for crepes; creamed chicken or crepes Suzette are two excellent examples. They are also terrific as an unusual variation on beef or chicken Tostadas (see recipe, page 156). If you have extra pancakes left over, freeze them tightly wrapped in foil.

CREPE BATTER:

2 LARGE EGGS

1 CUP MILK

2 TABLESPOONS MOLASSES

¼ TEASPOON SALT

½ TEASPOON GROUND GINGER

½ TEASPOON GROUND CLOVES

½ TEASPOON GROUND CINNAMON

¼ TEASPOON GROUND NUTMEG

1 CUP UNBLEACHED OR WHITE
   PRESIFTED ALL-PURPOSE FLOUR

4½ TABLESPOONS UNSALTED
   BUTTER

FILLING:

¾ CUP SPREADABLE BLUEBERRIES
   (SUCH AS POLANER ALL FRUIT)

¾ CUP FRESH BLUEBERRIES

CONFECTIONERS' SUGAR

Whisk together the eggs, milk, molasses, salt, ginger, cloves, cinnamon, and nutmeg. Whisk in the flour until smooth, then pour into a large measuring cup with a spout.

Heat a 6″ skillet or crepe pan over medium heat. Melt 2 teaspoons of the butter in the pan. Pour in one thirteenth of the batter (about 2 tablespoons), just enough to cover the entire bottom of the skillet. Immediately swirl the batter around to make an even layer. If you've poured in too much, quickly pour the excess back into the measuring cup. Cook for 30 to 60 seconds, until ½″ of the batter around the edges is completely cooked. Flip with a spatula and cook the other side just until no longer damp. You will probably discard this pancake—or eat it yourself —since the first one never comes out right.

Make the remaining crepes the same way, adding more butter to the skillet as necessary to prevent sticking. As the crepes are finished, stack them and let them cool. You'll probably use a total of 1½ tablespoons of butter for frying.

Place a cooled crepe, second side up, in front of you. Arrange 1 table-spoon spreadable fruit in a row about 1″ down from one of the sides, then spreading to ½″ from the 2 adjoining sides. Top with 1 tablespoon fresh blueberries, pressing them lightly into the spreadable fruit. Roll jelly-roll style, starting with the side nearest the filling, and let sit, seam side down. Form the remaining blintzes.

Melt 1½ tablespoons of butter in a medium-size skillet over medium heat. Add 4 blintzes and brown them lightly, turning once. Arrange 2 each on heated plates. Add half the remaining butter to the skillet and fry 4 more blintzes. Use the remaining butter for the last 4. Sprinkle the blintzes with confectioners' sugar and serve immediately.

**MAKES 12 BLINTZES**

This is almost the same batter used for Corn Dogs (see recipe page 149). Legend has it that hunters or fishermen tossed these to their dogs to quiet the hungry animals eyeing the men's campfire dinners. You can add grated Cheddar cheese to the batter, but be careful it doesn't burn. Traditionally, hush puppies are served alongside fried fish; I think that's a tradition to be preserved.

VEGETABLE OIL

¼ CUP YELLOW CORNMEAL

2 TABLESPOONS UNBLEACHED OR WHITE PRESIFTED ALL-PURPOSE FLOUR

2 TABLESPOONS WHOLE WHEAT FLOUR

¼ TEASPOON BAKING POWDER

¼ TEASPOON SALT

¼ TEASPOON GINGER

¼ TEASPOON CINNAMON

¼ TEASPOON CLOVES

1 LARGE EGG WHITE

5 TABLESPOONS MILK

1 ½ TEASPOONS PREPARED MUSTARD

1 TEASPOON MOLASSES

1 TABLESPOON HONEY

Pour the oil into a medium-size skillet to a depth of 1″ and heat to 300°F. Mix together the cornmeal, flours, baking powder, salt, ginger, cinnamon, and cloves.

In a separate bowl lightly whisk the egg white, milk, mustard, molasses, and honey together, then whisk into the dry ingredients until very smooth.

Drop tablespoons of the batter into the hot oil and fry until dark brown but not burnt or blackened. Drain on paper towels and serve immediately.

**MAKES ABOUT 18 HUSH PUPPIES**

While this can be made with just the gingerbread batter, it's four times as good with one of the ginger yeast breads included earlier in this chapter. Potato Bread, Whole Wheat Bread, or Brioches are my favorites. I prefer the bread thinly sliced, about ¼″ thick, but others may like it thicker. Lay an orange slice on each slice of French toast and judiciously top with Cider "Honey" (see recipe, page 93), maple syrup, or cinnamon sugar. As for me, I'm always disappointed if there's no bacon on the side.

2 LARGE EGGS

¼ TEASPOON GROUND GINGER

¼ TEASPOON GROUND CINNAMON

PINCH OF GROUND CLOVES

1 TABLESPOON BROWN SUGAR

2 TABLESPOONS BUTTER

4 SLICES OF BREAD, CUT ¼″–½″ THICK

Thoroughly whisk together the eggs, ginger, cinnamon, cloves, and brown sugar.

Melt 1 tablespoon butter in a skillet large enough to hold 2 slices of bread. Cut the remaining butter into quarters.

Dip 2 slices of bread, one at a time, into the batter, turning to coat both sides evenly. Immediately place the bread in the skillet. Fry, turning once, until both sides are lightly browned. Whenever the butter in the pan begins to brown, add a piece of the remaining butter. Fry the other 2 bread slices and serve immediately.

**SERVES 2**

# SAVORY DISHES

**W**hen most people think of savory gingerbread recipes, the first—and probably only—one that comes to mind is sauerbraten in gingersnap gravy. There are, however, many, many more. Eastern Europe has a whole repertoire of dishes thickened with gingerbread cake, cookies, or gingersnaps. Tongue in raisin sauce, jugged rabbit, venison, pork roast, ham, beef stew, cabbage soup, and all the traditional Christmas Eve carp dishes are delightfully gingery, sweet and sour.

I've now added to the range of gingersnap dishes, some using spicy crumbs, others employing savory ginger breads or pastry. I hope these inspire you to think of others. Any dish that would be improved by ginger and can take a little sweetening is a perfect candidate. Try a gingersnap curry, or use one part gingersnap or ginger graham crumbs to three parts regular bread crumbs as a coating for fried fish, especially Chinese-style.

Several of the recipes below call for leftovers from previous chapters. My theory is that it's always easier to make a lot at one time than to bake twice. That's why I usually make two loaves of bread, several dozen cookies, or extra blintz pancakes and keep them in the freezer. Since many commercial gingersnaps are somewhat harsh, buy gingerbread cookies instead if you don't have time to bake. The ginger corn bread or blintzes used in this chapter can't be bought, of course. But if you serve the chicken with corn bread stuffing or the tostadas the day after you've served the bread or blintzes, I don't think anyone will mind.

# SAUERBRATEN
## WITH GINGERSNAP GRAVY

Sauerbraten, along with sauerkraut, sausages, and dumplings, symbolizes German food to Americans. This recipe calls for the meat to marinate at least forty-eight hours. Don't shorten the marinating time; the vinegar contributes both taste and tenderness to the meat. I make a very thick gravy, so if you prefer it lighter, add only five tablespoons of gingersnap crumbs. Traditional accompaniments are red cabbage and boiled potatoes, potato pancakes with applesauce, potato or cracker dumplings, or spaetzle. Thick egg noodles, sauerkraut, and mashed potatoes are also delicious with this.

1 3–4-POUND BOTTOM ROUND OF BEEF

1 TEASPOON SALT

2 GARLIC CLOVES, CRUSHED WELL

3 JUNIPER BERRIES

2 WHOLE CLOVES

6 BLACK PEPPERCORNS

2 CUPS WATER

1 CUP CIDER VINEGAR

1 CUP WHITE OR WINE VINEGAR

1 ONION, THINLY SLICED

2 BAY LEAVES, BROKEN IN HALF

3 TABLESPOONS VEGETABLE OIL

2 TABLESPOONS BACON FAT, LARD, OR ADDITIONAL VEGETABLE OIL

7 TABLESPOONS FINELY CRUSHED GINGERSNAPS OR CRUMBLED BASIC GINGERBREAD CAKE (PAGE 25 OR 52)

Place the meat in a deep glass or enamel dish. Rub it all over with the salt and garlic.

Coarsely crush the juniper berries, cloves, and peppercorns in a mortar. In a large saucepan bring the crushed berry mixture, water, vinegars, onion, bay leaves, and 3 tablespoons oil just to a boil. Immediately remove from the heat and pour over the meat. Turn the meat to coat it with the liquid. Cover the dish and refrigerate for 2 to 4 days. Turn the meat once or twice a day.

Remove the meat from the marinade and pat dry. In a Dutch oven heat the bacon fat, lard, or oil over a medium-high flame. Brown the meat on all sides, then add a ladle of the marinade. When it stops spattering, pour in the rest. Simmer, covered, without bringing to a boil, for 2 or 3 hours, until the meat is easily pierced with a fork. Turn once while it's cooking, about an hour into the cooking time.

Remove the meat from the pot and set aside. Strain 2 cups of the cooking liquid into a saucepan. Bring to a boil, add the ginger crumbs, and stir until the gravy thickens.

**MAKES 6 SERVINGS**

# QUICHE WITH GINGERBREAD PASTRY CRUST

Savory gingerbread pastry is very versatile. Potpies, Cornish pasties, and meat-filled empanadas are just a few possibilities. The dough can be frozen, tightly wrapped in plastic, for up to a month. You can use this crust for a traditional bacon and Gruyère quiche rather than this mix of sausage, Cheddar, and chile, but I like the way the strong flavors blend. Serve the quiche with a salad and a spicy white wine such as Gewürztraminer.

¼ POUND FRESH CRUMBLED GARLIC
   SAUSAGE WITHOUT CASINGS
½ MEDIUM ONION (ABOUT 10
   TABLESPOONS), ROUGHLY
   CHOPPED
1 SMALL FRESH CHILE, SEEDED AND
   FINELY CHOPPED (OPTIONAL)
2 TABLESPOONS VEGETABLE OIL (IF
   NECESSARY)

1 RECIPE SAVORY GINGERBREAD
   PASTRY (PAGE 145)
1 CUP TIGHTLY PACKED COARSELY
   GRATED SHARP CHEDDAR CHEESE
4 LARGE EGGS
¼ TEASPOON SALT
⅛ TEASPOON WHITE PEPPER
½ CUP HEAVY CREAM

Heat a medium-size skillet over a medium flame. Crumble the sausage into the skillet. As soon as the sausage begins releasing its fat, add the onion and chile. Sauté until the meat is browned completely, constantly breaking up lumps of meat with the side of a fork or spoon. Add up to 2 tablespoons oil if the ingredients stick to the skillet. Remove with a slotted spoon and drain on paper towels. Cool to room temperature.

Preheat the oven to 375°F. Roll the pastry dough out into a ¼″-thick circle. You'll probably need to pick it up in pieces to place in an 8″ pie pan, since it's slightly crumbly. Just press the pieces together so they appear seamless. Flute or otherwise decorate the edges of the piecrust. Freeze any excess dough for use another time. Prick the crust all over with the tines of a fork.

Scatter the sausage mixture over the bottom of the crust. Top with ½ cup cheese. Whisk together the eggs, salt, white pepper, and heavy cream until frothy. Pour into the pan, evenly covering the meat and cheese. Sprinkle on the remaining cheese.

Bake for 40 minutes, or until the top is puffed all over and a skewer inserted into the middle of the quiche comes out clean. If the crust browns too quickly, cover it with foil. Serve hot or at room temperature.

**MAKES 6 SERVINGS**

## SAVORY GINGERBREAD PASTRY

1 ½ CUPS UNBLEACHED OR WHITE
    PRESIFTED ALL-PURPOSE FLOUR
1 TEASPOON GROUND GINGER
1 TEASPOON GROUND CINNAMON
¼ TEASPOON GROUND CLOVES
¼ TEASPOON GROUND NUTMEG

½ TEASPOON SALT
¼ CUP BROWN SUGAR
3 LARGE EGG YOLKS
1 TABLESPOON MOLASSES
½ CUP UNSALTED BUTTER, MELTED
    AND COOLED

Mix together the flour, ginger, cinnamon, cloves, nutmeg, salt, and brown sugar in a large bowl. Make a well in the center. Whisk together the yolks, molasses, and butter, then pour into the well. Using a fork, stir the flour mixture into the liquid, beginning with the dry ingredients adjacent to the well. When it's almost completely incorporated, turn the dough out and knead several times just until smooth. Refrigerate, tightly wrapped in plastic, for at least 30 minutes.

# CHICKEN WITH
## GINGER—CORN BREAD STUFFING

Since corn bread doesn't keep very well, this recipe is perfect for left-overs. It uses roughly a quarter recipe of Ginger Corn Bread. If you want to cheat, you can use regular corn bread and add crushed and minced fresh ginger to the stuffing mixture. Half-inch cubes of stale Potato Bread or Whole Wheat Bread (see recipe, page 112 or 114) can be substituted for the corn bread. My favorite side dishes with the chicken are garlicky stir-fried mixed vegetables or real southern greens, simmered for hours with a ham hock.

7½ TABLESPOONS UNSALTED
BUTTER
1 MEDIUM LEEK, WHITE AND LIGHT
GREEN PART ONLY, COARSELY
CHOPPED
3 CUPS COARSELY CHOPPED FRESH
WHITE OR WILD MUSHROOMS
1½ CUPS ROUGHLY CRUMBLED
GINGER CORN BREAD (PAGE
116)
¼ CUP WATER CHESTNUTS, CUT INTO
⅛"–¼" CUBES

1 LARGE EGG
2 TABLESPOONS MILK OR CHICKEN
STOCK
SALT AND PEPPER TO TASTE
1 3½-POUND WHOLE CHICKEN
1 TABLESPOON HONEY
2 TEASPOONS PREPARED MUSTARD
COUPLE DASHES OF
WORCESTERSHIRE SAUCE

Preheat the oven to 450°F. Melt 4½ tablespoons of the butter in a medium-size saucepan. Add the leek and mushrooms and stir just until they're completely moistened with the butter. Pour out into a large bowl and fold in the corn bread and water chestnuts. Whisk together the egg and milk or stock, then fold into the bowl. Season with salt and pepper.

Stuff the chicken without packing it tightly. Close the chicken with toothpicks or metal skewers. Place, breast side up, on an oiled rack set in a roasting pan.

Roast the chicken for 10 minutes. Turn the heat down to 350°, and cook for 20 minutes more. While the chicken cooks, melt the remaining 3 tablespoons of butter in a small saucepan. Stir in the honey, mustard, and Worcestershire. Turn off the heat, but leave the pan on the burner, covered. It must be reheated about 1 minute before you use it each time.

After the first 30 minutes (10 minutes at 450° plus 20 minutes at 350°), brush the chicken with two-thirds of the honey mixture. Turn the chicken over and cook for 30 minutes more. Brush with half the remaining honey mixture and any pan drippings. Cook for 20 minutes more, then brush with the rest of the honey mixture and any drippings. Turn the chicken breast side up and cook for 10 minutes more. The total cooking time is 10 minutes at 450°, then 80 minutes at 350°. Remove the chicken from the oven and let sit for 5 minutes before carving.

**MAKES 4 SERVINGS**

The mushroom stuffing can be made a day ahead, without the crumbs, and refrigerated. Just before broiling the mushrooms, gently warm the filling mixture and stir in the cookie crumbs. You can replace the crab with minced ham, shrimp, or any kind of smoked fish, so it's a perfect recipe for using up leftovers. If you stumble upon fresh water chestnuts, rather than canned, by all means buy them. When peeled, they are delicious enough to eat like candy. They'll also improve any recipe to which they're added.

**3 TABLESPOONS UNSALTED BUTTER**

**½ CUP TIGHTLY PACKED SHREDDED COOKED CRABMEAT**

**3 TABLESPOONS FINELY CHOPPED WATER CHESTNUTS**

**4 TEASPOONS MINCED LEEK WHITE**

**½ CUP FINELY CHOPPED RAW BROCCOLI FLORETS**

**3 TABLESPOONS CHICKEN STOCK**

**4 TEASPOONS GROUND GINGERSNAPS OR MACAROONS (PAGE 25 OR 44)**

**20—25 FRESH MUSHROOMS, EACH ABOUT 1 ½″ —2″ IN DIAMETER, STEMS REMOVED**

Preheat the broiler. Melt 2 tablespoons of the butter in a medium-size skillet over low heat. Sauté the crab, water chestnuts, leek, and broccoli for 2 to 3 minutes. Turn off the heat and stir in the stock and ginger crumbs. Set the pan aside.

Melt the remaining butter and brush the mushroom caps with it. Broil, stem side down, for 2 minutes.

Turn the mushrooms stem side up and stuff each with about 2 teaspoons of the crab mixture. The filling will be slightly mounded. Place the mushrooms on a baking sheet. Broil until the crab is lightly browned on top, which takes from 2 to 5 minutes, depending on your broiler. Cool for 1 minute before serving.

**MAKES 20 TO 25 MUSHROOMS**

Gingerbread flavorings make corn dogs a lot more exciting. Be sure you buy the best hot dogs you can find, since there's no point in going to the trouble of making corn dogs if a gelatinous hot dog will ruin the taste anyway. If a similar batter is dropped by tablespoons into hot oil, you'll get Hush Puppies (see recipe, page 136).

VEGETABLE OIL

¼ CUP YELLOW CORNMEAL

2 TABLESPOONS UNBLEACHED OR
   WHITE PRESIFTED ALL-PURPOSE
   FLOUR

2 TABLESPOONS WHOLE WHEAT
   FLOUR

¼ TEASPOON BAKING POWDER

¼ TEASPOON SALT

¼ TEASPOON GROUND GINGER

¼ TEASPOON GROUND CINNAMON

¼ TEASPOON GROUND CLOVES

1 LARGE EGG WHITE

6 TABLESPOONS MILK

1½ TEASPOONS PREPARED MUSTARD

1 TEASPOON MOLASSES

8 HOT DOGS

Pour the oil into a large skillet to a depth of 2″ and heat to 350°F. Mix together the cornmeal, flours, baking powder, salt, ginger, cinnamon, and cloves in a large bowl. Whisk together the egg white, milk, mustard, and molasses, then whisk into the dry ingredients until very smooth.

When the oil is hot, drop 2 hot dogs into the batter and turn to coat evenly. Gently lift out with tongs, letting the excess batter drip back into the bowl. Carefully place in the oil and fry, turning with tongs once or twice if necessary, 3 or 4 minutes, until crispy and browned all over. Drain on paper towels. Make the rest of the corn dogs the same way.

**MAKES 8 CORN DOGS**

Adapted from a definitive nineteenth-century English cookbook called *The Book of Household Management*, by Mrs. Beeton, this is old-fashioned mincemeat made with ground beef. You can omit the beef, but I think it adds richness to the recipe. While many recipes call for suet, a type of beef fat, regular ground beef has just enough fat to make perfect mincemeat. Refrigerated mincemeat keeps at least three weeks, so you can make it well in advance.

For dessert, bake the mincemeat in large or small Gingerbread Tartlet Shells (see recipe, page 86). While I usually prefer to make my own tomato sauce, if I don't have time I use an excellent sauce such as Classico tomato and basil or Prego tomato with fresh mushrooms.

| | |
|---|---|
| 2 POUNDS REGULAR GROUND BEEF | 2 TABLESPOONS ORANGE LIQUEUR |
| 2 LARGE TART APPLES, PEELED AND GRATED | ¼ CUP BRANDY OR COGNAC |
| ½ CUP DARK RAISINS | GRATED RIND OF 2 LEMONS, PLUS ¼ CUP JUICE |
| ½ CUP YELLOW RAISINS | 6 5–6-OUNCE GREEN PEPPERS |
| ½ CUP FINELY CHOPPED DRIED APRICOTS | ½ CUP COARSELY CRUSHED GINGERSNAP CRUMBS (PAGE 25) |
| ½ TEASPOON SALT | 2 CUPS VERY THICK TOMATO SAUCE |
| ¼ TEASPOON WHITE PEPPER | |

One to three weeks before using, make the mincemeat: Toss the beef, apples, raisins, and apricots in a large bowl. In a separate bowl mix together the salt, pepper, liqueur, brandy, and lemon rind and juice, and knead into the meat mixture. Pack into a crock or wrap tightly in plastic and refrigerate.

Preheat the oven to 375°F. Grease two 10″ round baking dishes or any other size dish that will hold the peppers close together in one layer. Bring a large pot of water to a boil. Halve the peppers lengthwise, discarding the stems and seeds. Drop into the water and boil for 5 minutes. Drain well and pat dry.

Divide the mincemeat into 12 parts and stuff the pepper halves. The filling will be mounded. Sprinkle with the crumbs, pressing them gently into the mincemeat with your fingertips. Arrange the peppers in the baking dishes; it's all right if the peppers touch slightly. Pour half the tomato sauce into each dish, around, not on top of, the peppers. Bake for 40 minutes.

**Makes 6 servings as a main course, 12 as a side dish**

While most people think apple when they think strudel, savory strudels are equally loved in eastern Europe. Replacing the usual bread crumbs with gingersnap turns everyday cabbage and bacon into something special. If you have a German delicatessen nearby, I strongly recommend using their double-smoked bacon. Many European-style delis also sell strudel dough. Fresh or frozen phyllo pastry dough, an acceptable substitute, is sold in Middle Eastern groceries and some supermarkets. The cookies are also delicious in fruit or cheese strudels. Although usually considered a side dish, this is a perfect main course on a cold winter evening. Along with a mug of soup, and Pear Brown Betty or a hot Baked Apple (see recipe, page 95 or 85) with a glass of port for dessert, it's unbeatably soothing.

1 2-POUND HEAD OF CABBAGE, CORED, SHREDDED OR GRATED

SMALL HANDFUL OF COARSE, KOSHER, OR SEA SALT

½ TEASPOON WHITE PEPPER

1 ¼ TEASPOONS CARAWAY SEEDS

½ POUND BACON, COARSELY CHOPPED

1 ½ CUPS FINELY CHOPPED ONIONS

1 ½ CUPS ROUGHLY CHOPPED FRESH WHITE OR WILD MUSHROOMS

4 SHEETS OF STRUDEL OR PHYLLO PASTRY DOUGH

10 TEASPOONS UNSALTED BUTTER, MELTED

6 TABLESPOONS FINELY CRUSHED GINGERSNAP CRUMBS (PAGE 25)

Toss the cabbage with the salt, place in a colander, and let sit in the sink for 30 minutes. Then squeeze out the moisture, pat dry, and place in a large bowl. Toss with the pepper and caraway seeds.

In a skillet cook the bacon over medium heat until almost crisp. Remove with a slotted spoon, drain on paper towels, then crumble into the cabbage. Sauté the onions in the bacon fat for 5 minutes. Add the mushrooms to the skillet and cook for 3 or 4 minutes more. Pour the contents of the skillet into the cabbage bowl and toss well.

Preheat the oven to 400°F. Grease a baking sheet. Lay out a sheet of the strudel or phyllo dough on your work surface. Brush it with about 2 teaspoons of the melted butter. Sprinkle evenly with about 1½ tablespoons of the gingersnap crumbs. Repeat the layers 3 times, until all the dough and crumbs have been used.

Spoon the cabbage mixture onto the top sheet of strudel in a rectangle, leaving 1″ dough uncovered on all sides. Starting with a long side, roll up the strudel like a jelly roll. Carefully set it on the baking sheet seam side down. Brush with the remaining 2 teaspoons butter. Bake for 35 minutes or until golden brown. Remove from the oven and let rest for 10 minutes before cutting. Serve with mustard.

**MAKES 6 SERVINGS AS A MAIN COURSE, 10 AS A SIDE DISH**

There's nothing better than a great meat loaf and nothing worse than a bland one, so I mix in lots of onion, celery, peppers, ketchup, Worcestershire sauce, fresh herbs and, of course, ginger-flavored crumbs. You can use Ginger Graham Cracker, Potato or Whole Wheat Bread crumbs (see recipe, page 128, 112, or 114), replacing the bread crumbs in your meat loaf recipe or the gingersnap crumbs in mine. There's no better accompaniment to meat loaf than mashed potatoes or even Gingersnap-Coated Potato Croquettes (see recipe, page 158). Any kind of green vegetable, as long as it's not overcooked, completes your main course. Serve any leftover meat loaf in a sandwich made with the ginger Whole Wheat Bread.

4 STRIPS OF BACON, COARSELY CHOPPED

¾ TEASPOON GROUND DRIED CHILES (NOT CHILI POWDER) OR PAPRIKA

1 CUP COARSELY CHOPPED ONION

½ CUP COARSELY CHOPPED CELERY

1 CUP COARSELY CHOPPED RED BELL PEPPER

2 POUNDS LEAN GROUND BEEF

¼ CUP PLUS 3 TABLESPOONS KETCHUP

1 ½ TEASPOONS WORCESTERSHIRE SAUCE

1 TEASPOON SALT

½ TEASPOON BLACK PEPPER

½ CUP GINGERSNAP CRUMBS (PAGE 25)

2 LARGE EGGS, LIGHTLY BEATEN

¼ CUP TIGHTLY PACKED FINELY CHOPPED FRESH BASIL OR OREGANO (OPTIONAL—DON'T USE DRIED)

In a skillet cook the bacon over medium heat until the fat is rendered out. Add the chiles, onion, celery, and bell pepper. Cook, stirring often, for 7 to 8 minutes, until most of the fat is gone and the vegetables begin to stick to the bottom of the pan. Remove the pan from the heat.

While the vegetables are cooking, mix together the meat, ¼ cup ketchup, Worcestershire sauce, salt, pepper, gingersnaps, eggs, and basil in a large bowl. Preheat the oven to 350°F. Scrape the skillet's contents into the meat mixture and mix well. Pack lightly in an 8½"-x-4½" glass loaf pan.

Bake for 30 minutes. Spread the top of the meat loaf with the remaining 3 tablespoons ketchup and bake for 40 minutes more. Serve hot.

**MAKES 6 SERVINGS**

This recipe was created when, longing for a light, easy, one-dish meal, I discovered one leftover ginger blintz crepe and a small amount of leftover roast beef in the freezer. Mexican food came to mind, and this was the result. Now I always make several extra crepes especially for this dish. The crepes can be fried up to a week ahead and reheated; they won't be crisp but can be picked up and eaten with your hands like soft tacos. Almost anything goes on these, and some of my friends think the tostadas are incomplete without refried beans between the crepes and lettuce. Try to find a spicy salsa, and taste it to determine whether the tostada requires any more onions.

4 COOLED CREPES (⅓ BLUEBERRY BLINTZES RECIPE, PAGE 134)

TASTELESS VEGETABLE OIL (SUCH AS WESSON)

2 CUPS COOKED BEEF, CHICKEN, OR PORK, CUT INTO SMALL BITE-SIZE PIECES

½ CUP FINELY CHOPPED RIPE TOMATO

¼ CUP MINCED ONION (OPTIONAL)

2 CUPS SHREDDED CRISP LETTUCE

½ CUP GUACAMOLE

1 CUP SHREDDED SHARP CHEDDAR CHEESE

½ CUP SALSA, VERY THICK OR DRAINED IN A SIEVE BEFORE USING

In a skillet just large enough to hold one crepe, pour the oil to a depth of 1″. Heat over a high flame. Fry the crepes, one at a time, until very brown. Drain on paper towels, then place each on a plate.

Reheat the meat until warm or hot, depending on your taste, while the crepes are frying. Toss the tomato and onion together.

Top each crepe in the following order, leaving a ½″ border uncovered all around. First scatter ½ cup of the lettuce over each. Top with ½ cup of the meat, then 2 tablespoons of the tomato and onion. Add 2 tablespoons of the guacamole, then ¼ cup of the cheese, then 2 tablespoons of the salsa. Serve at once.

MAKES 4 TOSTADAS

# WALNUT BREAD CROUTES
## WITH CHEESE AND
## SUN-DRIED TOMATOES

While this sounds like an American nouvelle cuisine cliché, it's very delicious and very easy. Since it's so simple, the taste of the raw ingredients is very important. Don't use a delicate olive oil; it must be very fruity, like the inexpensive Greek variety. You can use a slightly crumbly soft cheese, such as goat cheese, if you microwave it briefly to make it spreadable. I prefer the tasty spreadable cheeses (Boursin or Rondelé, for example) available in supermarkets, since they can be used as is. When you buy sun-dried tomatoes, try to find the ones packed in oil with garlic and herbs. They're softer and tastier than the dry-packed ones.

FRUITY OLIVE OIL

8 ½"-THICK SLICES OF SAVORY
  ONION-WALNUT QUICK BREAD
  (PAGE 117), EACH CUT INTO 4
  TRIANGLES

¾ CUP CRUMBLED SOFT CHEESE, AT
  ROOM TEMPERATURE

32 SMALL SUN-DRIED TOMATO
  HALVES

½ CUP SHREDDED FRESH BASIL

In a medium-size skillet pour the oil to a depth of ½". Heat until an extra piece of bread dropped into the oil immediately begins to sizzle. Fry the triangles, 4 at a time, for 30 to 40 seconds on each side, until browned. Remove with a slotted spoon and drain well on paper towels. Fry and drain the remaining triangles in batches of 4.

Cool them slightly to prevent the cheese from running. Then spread each with 1 heaping teaspoon of cheese, top with a tomato half, and sprinkle with basil.

**MAKES 32 CROUTES**

# GINGERSNAP-
## COATED POTATO CROQUETTES

While gingersnaps and potatoes may seem a somewhat odd combination, let these change your mind. They are slightly sweet since cookies are used, but that makes them the perfect foil for a spicy main course. Serve with Indian curries, Mexican meat dishes, American barbecue, or a great meat loaf. Freeze the unbaked croquettes spread on a greased baking sheet, not touching each other, until hard. Then store them in a plastic bag. That way you can remove only as many as you need, since they won't stick together. Reheat them by frying as you would fresh ones, then microwave on high until the inside is hot. You can also bake the frozen croquettes 25 minutes at 350°F., but they won't be as crisp as the fried/microwaved ones.

| | |
|---|---|
| 4 MEDIUM BAKING POTATOES (ABOUT 2½ POUNDS TOTAL) | 1 TEASPOON SALT |
| 2 TABLESPOONS UNSALTED BUTTER, AT ROOM TEMPERATURE | ½ TEASPOON WHITE PEPPER |
| 3 LARGE EGGS | ¼ CUP UNBLEACHED OR WHITE FLOUR |
| ¾ CUP FIRMLY PACKED SHREDDED SHARP CHEDDAR CHEESE | 1½ CUPS GROUND GINGERSNAPS (PAGE 25) |
| 3 TABLESPOONS SHREDDED FRESH BASIL (OPTIONAL) | TASTELESS VEGETABLE OIL (SUCH AS WESSON) |

Boil the potatoes until tender. Peel them, then rice, sieve, or mash them in a bowl. Beat in the butter. Cool to room temperature, or refrigerate overnight.

Beat 1 egg, the cheese, basil, salt, and pepper into the potatoes. Then stir in the flour just until incorporated.

Pick up a handful of the potato mixture and squeeze to compress and smooth it. Roll between your palms to create a log 1″ wide and 3″ long. Return any excess to the bowl. Make the rest of the logs the same way.

In a small bowl whisk the remaining eggs to break up completely. Place the gingersnaps in a second bowl. In a medium-size skillet pour the oil to a depth of 1″ and heat to 350°F.

Drop a log into the egg, then remove, letting any excess drip back into the bowl. Roll in the crumbs to coat evenly and completely. Set on a baking sheet while you coat the rest of the croquettes.

Drop 5 croquettes into the oil. Fry, turning once, until browned all over. Remove with a slotted spoon or tongs and drain on a paper towel. Fry the remaining croquettes in batches of 5, then drain. Serve hot.

**MAKES 20 CROQUETTES**

# THE
# CHRISTMAS
# SEASON
# CALENDAR

**I**f you spent a month traveling around the world, beginning on December 6 and returning home on January 7, you could be served a different special gingerbread almost every day of your trip. Here's a sample all-gingerbread calendar for those of us Christmas lovers who choose to celebrate all year long.

**JANUARY:** Begin aging honey for lebkuchen (Germany).

**FEBRUARY:** Photographs of entries must be submitted for *Woman's Day* magazine Christmas gingerbread house competition (USA).

**AUGUST:** Bake fruitcakes, which will be soaked in liqueur.

**24:** St. Bartholomew's Day—begin fattening your Christmas carp (Germany).

Bake lebkuchen bar cookies and store in airtight container (Germany).

**SEPTEMBER 20:** Pour a jigger of liqueur on each fruitcake.

**OCTOBER:** Bake pebbernødder (gingersnaps), which will keep for months (Denmark).

**20:** Pour a jigger of liqueur on each fruitcake.

**NOVEMBER 20:** Pour a jigger of liqueur on each fruitcake.

**25:** Begin baking spiced fruit breads, spice cookies, and cakes, continuing to bake until Christmas (Germany).

**30:** Bake Black Bun (spiced fruitcake) for New Year's Eve (Scotland).

Bake Twelfth Cake (spiced fruitcake) for Twelfth Night (England).

**DECEMBER:** Peddler's Village, Lahaska, Pennsylvania, gingerbread house competition (USA).

Visit Christmas fairs and eat gingerbread cakes and cookies (Germany).

**2:** Begin macerating fruit for Black Cake (Virgin Islands) or Dominica Christmas Cake (Caribbean).

**6:** St. Nicholas Day—serve lebkuchen spice ring cake glazed with pear molasses (Switzerland).

Give speculaas (spice cookies baked in molds) to well-behaved children on this feast day (Belgium and Holland).

Moisten Twelfth Cake with rum or brandy.

**11:** Begin making gingerbread house (USA—see recipe, pages 169–77).

**19:** Bake gingerbread cookie ornaments and dry out on racks until you're ready to trim the tree (USA).

**20:** Give away liqueured fruitcake gifts.

Moisten Twelfth Cake with rum or brandy.

Pepparkakor (very thin gingerbread cookies) and glogg (alcoholic punch) handed out at museums during Christmas season (Sweden—see recipe for cookies, page 166).

**22:** Bake Dominica Christmas Cake.

Bake Moravian Christmas Wafers cut into circles, half-moons, stars, men, or animals (Pennsylvania, North Carolina, Virgin Islands, Germany).

**23:** Make Winter Spice Cake, which must be left outside for two days before serving (Switzerland).

Bake Black Cake.

Pour rum over Dominica Cake.

**24:** Pour rum over Dominica Cake.

Bake pepparkakor: also dried fruit–filled spice breads (Alsace, Germany) and pumpernickel bread with gingerbread cookie on top as decoration (Finland).

Serve carp in sweet-and-sour gingersnap sauce (Germany, Switzerland, Poland, Czechoslovakia) or carp in prune and gingersnap black sauce (Czechoslovakia), since Christmas Eve is traditionally meatless.

**25:** Christmas—serve Winter Spice Cake, Black Cake in one-inch squares, and Dominica Christmas Cake.

Serve each family member a pile of cookies, rolls, and pastries including pepparkakor (Sweden).

Serve pepparkakor wreath-shaped cookies and coffee after dinner (Finland).

Bake and serve Sweet Bread, an almond, orange peel, fruit, and spice bread (Virgin Islands); also serve Christmas spiced fruitcake (England —see recipe, page 167); baked and steamed spiced fruited pound cake (West Indies); and lebkuchentorte, a spiced honey cake (Germany).

**26:** Bake glogg cake (apple ginger cake) made with leftover fruits from the glogg punch (Sweden).

**31:** New Year's Eve—bake and serve Appenzell spiced honey cake (Switzerland) and sugared gingerbread slices with tea and honey (Russia).

Serve Black Bun.

Serve carp in gingersnap sauce, since New Year's Eve, Silvester, is also traditionally meatless (Germany).

**JANUARY 3:** Bake three fruitcakes in loaf pans for Kings' Day (Virgin Islands—see recipe, page 167).

**6:** Kings' Day, Twelfth Night, Epiphany—Twelfth Cake raffled off by bakeries (Dickens's England)

Serve three loaves of fruitcake. The man who finds the bean in his portion of a spice cake is elected king of the next party (New Orleans) or Lord of Misrule (France).

No gingerbread Christmas chapter would be complete without a description of the various printed and molded northern European cookies, especially those from Germany. Some of the cookies contain ginger, others cinnamon, anise, or other spices, but the doughs can often be used interchangeably in the different molds. The origins of these often elaborately designed cookies go back thousands of years. It's said that those too poor to provide the gods with an animal sacrifice would offer a cookie or bread shaped as an animal instead. In the Middle Ages, the cookies grew more elaborate, sometimes as tall as six feet, often depicting religious scenes. Cloistered monks were the most well-known mold makers, honoring each saint on his or her day as well as providing molds for every other religious holiday. Hosts would flatter a guest with a portrait of the visitor, and the upper classes vied to have their image produced by master bakers.

Many of the old molds still exist today, and some are still in use. The pictures range from the religious—the visiting Magi, the Madonna and Child, and a gathering of angels—to the humorous—St. Nicholas's donkey's droppings. Paler doughs could be painted with food coloring to create a soft, chalk- or watercolor-type drawing.

The following is a guide to the most famous molded or printed cookies:

SPECULAAS,   delicious butter and spice cookies, are made in molds that have only one impression in them. They range from a few inches high to six feet tall. The most popular cookie in both Belgium and Holland, they are an integral part of Christmas, often depicting St. Nicholas. In Germany they are called Rhineland spekulatius.

SPRINGERLE   are made with a special carved rolling pin or board with several repeats of the design on it. When these appear in the bakeries, German children know Christmas is near. These cookies are usually very pale and flavored with anise rather than ginger. Modern versions are often tasteless and less detailed than those from past centuries.

NÜRNBERG LEBKUCHEN   are pressed into large molds or baked as bars or cakes. They've been popular for hundreds of years and get their rich brown color from the local honey. The cookies are usually decorated with white icing, often including verses or the recipient's name. These cakes are also popular as Valentine gifts, baked as extremely large hearts.

Other Christmas gingerbread cookies are German aachener and Frankfurt printen, which are lightly pressed into molds so that designs appear "printed" on them, and Welsh ginger macaroons, which have been pressed into molds sprinkled with cinnamon sugar.

## SWEDISH PEPPARKAKOR

These very thin, brittle cookies have even more of a snap than ginger-snaps; cardamom gives them their unique Scandinavian flavor. Many shapes are popular, but hearts, five- or six-pointed stars, pigs, wreaths, Christmas trees, and men are traditional favorites. Often the children's favorite, the pigs, will have each child's name written on them with icing. While ammonium carbonate rather than baking soda is usually used for crispness, either one is fine. This dough is also used for gingerbread houses in Scandinavia.

| | |
|---|---|
| 2 TEASPOONS GROUND GINGER | ½ CUP UNSALTED BUTTER |
| 2 TEASPOONS GROUND CLOVES | ¼ CUP BROWN SUGAR |
| 1 TEASPOON GROUND CINNAMON | ¼ CUP DARK CORN SYRUP |
| ¾ TEASPOON GROUND CARDAMOM | ¼ CUP HEAVY CREAM |
| 2 TEASPOONS BAKING SODA (OR AMMONIUM CARBONATE) | 2 CUPS UNBLEACHED OR WHITE PRESIFTED ALL-PURPOSE FLOUR |

Preheat the oven to 325°F. Grease your baking sheets. Mix together the ginger, cloves, cinnamon, cardamom, and baking soda and set aside.

In a small saucepan, stirring often, heat the butter, sugar, corn syrup, and cream over very low heat until the butter is melted and the sugar has dissolved. Remove from the heat and beat in the spice mixture. Beat in the flour until well mixed. Wrap the mixture well in plastic and refrigerate until very firm, at least 4 hours.

On a lightly floured board, roll out half the dough until 1/16″ thick, leaving the remainder of the dough refrigerated. Cut into shapes using cookie cutters dipped into flour. Carefully transfer the cookies to the baking sheet with a spatula, placing them ½″ apart.

When all the cookies are on the baking sheets, pat or brush lightly with water. Bake for 14 minutes, until the edges are brown and the puffiness has gone down. Immediately transfer to racks to cool.

**MAKES 60 COOKIES**

I know, I know, most people hate fruitcakes. I do, myself, but this one is *really* different. Using brandy judiciously, rather than drowning the cake, helps a lot. You must also use dried and candied fruit good enough to eat plain, not the sickly sweet overprocessed stuff often sold as "mixed candied fruit." I use dark and golden raisins, roughly chopped figs and apricots, homemade candied orange, and good store-bought candied citron. Add any fruit you think would be appropriate. Candied ginger; liqueur-macerated fruit; fruit preserves; dried peaches and pears; and fresh orange, lemon, or tangerine peel are all wonderful in this.

Fruit-and-spice cakes are traditionally served at British and Caribbean weddings as well as at Christmastime, and I think this would be perfect as an unusual American wedding cake. Bake the layers in deep, round pans, then drape each with a thin layer of marzipan before decorating it. Add ¼ cup unsweetened cocoa powder plus 2 tablespoons strong coffee (liquid) to one or two of the layers for contrast.

2 CUPS COARSELY CHOPPED MIXED
  DRIED FRUIT

7 OUNCES CHOPPED CANDIED FRUIT

1 CUP COARSELY CHOPPED WALNUTS
  OR PECANS

2 CUPS UNBLEACHED OR WHITE
  PRESIFTED ALL-PURPOSE FLOUR

1½ TEASPOONS GROUND GINGER

1½ TEASPOONS GROUND CINNAMON

¼ TEASPOON GROUND NUTMEG

¼ TEASPOON GROUND CLOVES

1 TEASPOON BAKING SODA

½ TEASPOON SALT

½ CUP UNSALTED BUTTER

½ CUP MOLASSES

½ CUP BROWN SUGAR

2 TABLESPOONS BRANDY OR COGNAC

1 TABLESPOON ORANGE LIQUEUR

GRATED RIND OF 1 ORANGE

4 LARGE EGGS

Preheat the oven to 275°F. Grease an 8½"-x-4½" loaf pan. Toss the dried and candied fruit with the nuts and 2 tablespoons of the flour and set aside. Mix together the ginger, cinnamon, nutmeg, cloves, baking soda, and salt and set aside.

Melt the butter in a small saucepan. Remove from the heat and stir in the molasses and sugar. Scrape into a large bowl. Beat in the brandy or cognac, liqueur, orange rind, spice mixture, and then each egg, completely incorporating each ingredient before the next is added. Stir in the remaining flour. Fold in the fruit and nuts.

Pour the batter into the loaf pan. Bake for 2 hours, until a skewer inserted into the center comes out clean. The cake will keep for at least a month tightly wrapped in foil in the refrigerator or can be frozen for up to a year.

**MAKES 12 SERVINGS**

Last Christmas I finally made the house of my dreams: a 4′ wide by 3½′ deep Frank Lloyd Wright–style three-story castlelike abode. The entire house, along with its surrounding fences, the terraces, and roof, took about fourteen recipes of the gingerbread dough given below. The following directions, however, will work with any style and size of house. Each step is quite simple, and once you've made your first house, you'll realize that it's a lot easier than you thought.

Even if you plan to make only one gingerbread house in your life, there are a couple of specialized items worth buying. The first is a green or clear plastic cutting mat with a 1″ grid printed on it, available in art supply stores. If you roll the dough out on it, you can immediately see how big each piece of dough is without having to measure it. When you've finished the house, use the mat for cutting fabrics and various paper projects. I also have pairs of wooden dowels in various widths: $\frac{3}{16}$″, $\frac{1}{4}$″, $\frac{3}{8}$″, $\frac{7}{16}$″, and $\frac{1}{2}$″. I place a portion of dough on the floured cutting mat with a dowel (of the depth I want the dough to be) on either side. I roll the dough out until the rolling pin uses the dowels as tracks. This prevents you from rolling the dough out too thin. The dowels can be found at any good hardware or lumber store. They also sell L-shaped pieces of metal called angle irons or angle brackets, which I use to prop up the sides of the house while waiting for the icing "glue" to set. At Stampabarbara (see address on page 183), I found rubber stamps with which to make Tiffany-glass windows and doors and several geometric patterns that resembled cinder blocks and other building materials. Stamping the dough (without any dyes) before it's baked gives you a clear outline to paint in later.

This house is completely edible. If, however, you are sure that no one is going to eat it—and believe me, you may feel that way after all the love and care that go into it—there's a simple way to preserve it. Spray the house well inside and out with hair spray before the roof is put on. Every six months give the house another layer of spray on the outside, and it should last forever.

**FOR ONE BATCH OF DOUGH:**

5 TEASPOONS GROUND GINGER

2 1/2 TEASPOONS GROUND CINNAMON

1 TEASPOON GROUND CARDAMOM

1 TEASPOON GROUND NUTMEG

1/2 TEASPOON GROUND CLOVES

1 TEASPOON BAKING SODA

1/2 TEASPOON SALT

1 CUP UNSALTED BUTTER

1 1/2 CUPS MOLASSES

1 CUP WHITE SUGAR

1/4 CUP WATER

1 LARGE EGG

7 CUPS UNBLEACHED OR WHITE
   PRESIFTED ALL-PURPOSE FLOUR

FOOD COLORING (OPTIONAL)

**FOR ONE BATCH OF ICING:**

4 LARGE EGG WHITES

5 1/4 CUPS CONFECTIONERS' SUGAR

When you're ready to make your gingerbread house, the first step is to draw it on graph paper. If you map the house out very clearly at this point, you avoid problems later. Begin with a drawing of the shape of the house as seen from above (see Drawing 1). It's best not to have walls any wider or taller than 15″, since they won't fit on your baking sheet. If necessary, you can attach two sections of wall together, but it's a lot easier not to. Houses look best if they have lots of angles, which is why Victorians are always popular. Next, draw a picture of each façade of the house, also on graph paper (see Drawing 2). Then draw outlines of each wall (see Drawing 3). Wait until later to plot out the roof. Last of all, tape several pieces of graph paper to a solid wooden board such as Masonite or particle board and draw on a life-size outline of the house.

Since you don't know how much dough you'll need, make several batches—one at a time—and refrigerate each, wrapped in plastic, for at least 4 hours. The dough will keep up to a week in the refrigerator or can be frozen for six months. Mix together the ginger, cinnamon, cardamom, nutmeg, cloves, baking soda, and salt and set aside.

Melt the butter in a small saucepan. Remove from the heat, and stir in the molasses and sugar. Beat in the spice mixture completely, then the water, then the egg.

Place the flour in a large bowl and make a large well in the center. Pour the butter mixture into the well. Stir about a quarter of the flour, the part closest to the center, into the molasses mixture. Stir in half the remaining flour, then the rest. When all the flour has been incorporated, turn the dough out onto a board and knead just until smooth. Pat the dough out into a rectangle and wrap well. If the plastic opens and part of the dough dries out, wrap the dough in a wet paper towel for a couple of hours and it will be fine. If you like, you can add food coloring to batches of dough. If you dye the dough, make as much as you'll need all at once, since it's difficult to match the color later. Rose pink gives a nice adobe color, black creates a rich brown, and green is earthy looking.

Preheat the oven to 300°F. Remove one batch of dough from the refrigerator. Using the drawings of the walls as a guide, roll the dough out ⅛″ to ³⁄₁₆″ thick on a floured board, preferably one with a grid on it. Check off each wall on the graph paper as it's made. If you're using rubber stamps, press them firmly into the dough to mark the pattern. Stamp the doors and windows, then make a border along the bottom or top of the wall with the geometric print. This will stretch the dough, so, using a ruler or other straight object, push the edges of the dough back until it's the correct size. If it's a large piece of dough, gently roll it up on your rolling pin and unroll on a greased baking sheet or greased parchment atop a baking sheet. If you're using parchment, you can continue to prepare batches of dough on baking sheet–size sheets while the other batches are baking.

Bake the walls for 20 minutes if small, 25 minutes if large, until firm but not browned. Remove from the oven and carefully slide the walls off onto a cooling rack placed next to the baking sheet and at the same height. If the dough has risen so much you can hardly see the outlines of your stamps, stamp it once again immediately, while it's still soft. Continue to bake the remaining walls. If it's a large house, you can bake the walls over several days. When each wall has just cooled, measure it again. If it's larger than it should be, cut off the sides using a very sharp knife. Cool each wall on a rack for at least 2 days before it's used, since it hardens during that time. If a piece breaks off a wall, "glue" it back on with homemade or store-bought decorating icing.

The pieces of the house should be decorated before the house is put together. You can use a combination of different "paints." Use the egg yolks left over from the icing as a glaze, either lightly tinted with food coloring or in their slightly golden natural state. For less glossy colors, mix food coloring with some evaporated milk. I use both kinds of paint, as well as the decorating icings and writing gels available in the supermarket. There are kits with four different tips that can be screwed right onto the icing tubes. I like to glaze the entire house with natural yolk when it's completely painted, but it isn't necessary.

To put the house together, prepare one batch of icing at a time. Whisk together the egg whites and sugar for about 5 minutes, until smooth, thick, and very white. Then stir in some food coloring, a few drops at a time, if you want to match the dough. Build the house directly on the graph paper on the wooden board. It's easiest to attach the walls in groups of three (see Drawing 4), since they hold each other up. The L-shaped brackets will hold up any wobbly walls. Spread a thin layer of icing on the edge of a wall to attach it to the adjoining one. Then, when all three walls are in place, pipe a decorative pattern of icing down the connecting joints. Use writing gel to make a feathered pattern if you like, or leave the icing plain. Spoon any remaining icing into a container just large enough to hold it and press a piece of plastic wrap into the top. It will keep in the refrigerator for 2 to 3 days. The icing on the house will dry in about an hour, leaving the walls surprisingly solid. If you are planning to make a very tall house, put a flat roof on the second story, then build the third story atop that roof.

When all the walls have been put together, measure for the roof pieces in case some sections of the house are slightly larger or smaller than you planned. Add about ½″ extra of roof on all outer edges, not those adjoining another piece of roof, if you want an overhanging effect. Make and bake the roof pieces the same way as the walls, and cool them on a rack for at least a day.

If any of the walls are too high, carefully shave away the excess with a sharp knife. If a wall is too short, use any extra pieces of gingerbread you cut off when making the walls as shims. Spread a thin layer of icing on top of the walls and gently place on the roof pieces. Let dry until firm. Decorate the roof pieces after they've been placed atop the house. Use nuts, seeds, dried fruit, colored sugar, candied fruits, and anything else edible. Make another batch of icing, leaving it white. Spread it on the wooden board, covering the graph paper, so that it looks like a layer of snow. You can also make a gingerbread family and animals to go with the house, if you choose.

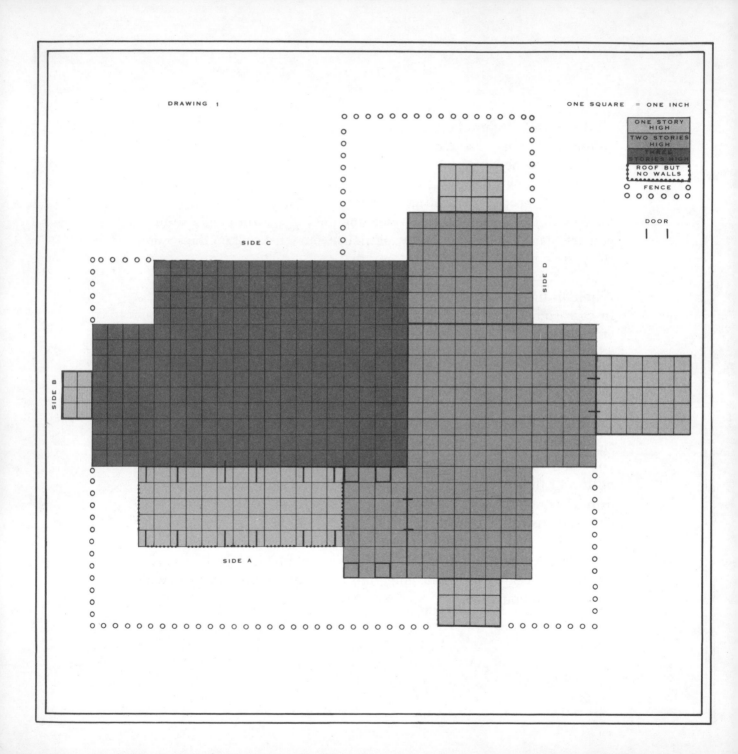

DRAWING 2

ONE SQUARE = ONE INCH

BALCONY
WALL

WALL E - - - - - - - - - - - - - - - - - - - - - - - - - - - - WALL F - - - -

WALL B - - - - - WALL C - - - - - - - - - - - - - -

WALL G

WALL A - - - - - - - -

WALL D

DRAWING 3

ONE SQUARE = ONE INCH

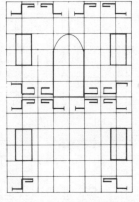

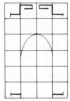

WALL C = 8 INCHES WIDE ×
12 INCHES HIGH

WALL D =
4 INCHES
WIDE ×
6 INCHES HIGH

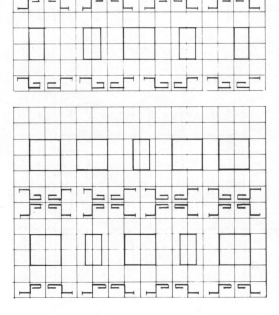

WALL E TO BE BAKED IN TWO PARTS

PART 1 (BOTTOM) = 16 INCHES WIDE × 12 INCHES HIGH

PART 2 (TOP) = 16 INCHES WIDE × 6 INCHES HIGH

DRAWING 4

ONE SQUARE = ONE INCH

ATTACH GROUP 1.

ATTACH GROUP 2 TOGETHER. THEN TO GROUP 1. LET SIT UNTIL DRY.

ATTACH GROUP 3 TOGETHER AND TO ADJOINING 1 WALL.

ATTACH GROUP 4 TO 3. LET SIT UNTIL DRY.

ATTACH GROUP 5 TOGETHER AND TO ADJOINING 3 WALL.

ATTACH GROUP 6 TOGETHER. THEN TO 5. LET SIT UNTIL DRY.

ATTACH GROUP 7 TO 1 AND 5 WALLS. LET SIT UNTIL DRY.

ATTACH GROUP 8 TOGETHER. THEN TO 7 WALLS.

ATTACH GROUP 9 TOGETHER. THEN TO GROUP 8. LET SIT UNTIL DRY.

# MAIL ORDER SOURCES

I have four excellent sources for both general and Christmas-oriented baking supplies, including ingredients as well as equipment. Following are sources that specialize in wonderful cookie molds and related items.

THE CHEF'S CATALOG says it sells "Professional Restaurant Equipment for the Home Chef," which is an accurate but not a complete description. The company also has lots of terrific gadgets. My favorite is the black steel oven pancake pan, which is perfect for Dutch apple pancakes. They carry four Cushion-Aire products: both sizes of baking sheets, the 9″ round cake pan, and the jelly-roll pan. They also sell several professional heavy-duty baking sheets and rolling pins, a cake-decorating kit with twelve tips, the Educated Cake Pan (rectangular pan with blocks that fit in it to make almost any shape of cake), springform cake pans, parchment, a spring-operated cake-decorating device with six tips, and three-sheet cookie mold sets with twelve indentations on each sheet, which can be used for sand tarts.

Every Christmas, the catalogue carries a selection of ceramic molds from both Brown Bag and Hartstone. In the past they've sold lambs, St. Nicholas, rabbits, teddy bears, foxes, and hearts. They also carry short-bread/springerle molds and a cast-iron plaque with a different style gingerbread house mold on each side. Contact: The Chef's Catalog, 3215 Commercial Avenue, Northbrook, IL 60062-1920; (800) 338-3232.

MAID OF SCANDINAVIA caters to both recreational cooks and professional bakeries, carrying everything a baker could possibly need. The company's catalogue is a joy, leaving any impressionable person (like me) pining for everything in it—including literally hundreds of different cake pans, ranging from cartoon characters to elaborate five-tiered wedding cakes. They also carry several different kinds of food colors, including those used in airbrushing, each in many colors; cake stands; every shape of tip for cake decorating; icing pens and gels and crayons; utilitarian and decorative cake boards; cake pan liners; figures for the tops of cakes; and other decorating tools, including spatulas, flower formers, icing smoothers, and ¼″-thick wooden dowels which can be used as a guide when rolling out dough. They stock all the Cushion-Aire baking pans; springform cake pans, including round, tube, and rectangular; two sizes of nonstick and regular Educated Cake

Pans; rectangular and round checkerboard cake pans; fattigmand cookie cutters and rollers; cannoli tubes; a trifle bowl; and various sizes of cooling racks.

Also available are many ready-made ingredients, including icing and cake mixes; instant fondant; caramel; coating sugars; ammonium carbonate; various flours; all kinds of fruit and other flavor extracts; and every kind of cake decoration, including sugar in orange, purple, pink, green, yellow, blue, and red; beautiful ready-made icing flowers and other shapes; and edible glitter. Christmas specialties include a mold for a small, solid gingerbread cake house; cake pans of Santa, a "Gingerbread Boy," a bell, star, or Christmas tree; a springerle board and rolling pin; an Art Deco cookie stamp set; ceramic cookie stamps with Christmas designs; hundreds of cookie cutters in Christmas and other shapes; gingerbread house and large men cookie cutters; and Santa and Hansel and Gretel lebkuchen cutters. Contact: Maid of Scandinavia, 3244 Raleigh Avenue, Minneapolis, MN 55416; (800) 328-6722.

**WILLIAMS-SONOMA** prefers the definitive to the comprehensive, and everything they carry is top-quality. Baking pans include the Educated Cake Pan, a round checkerboard cake pan, all four Cushion-Aire pans, and several sizes of both nonstick and regular round springform cake pans. They sell a variety of rolling pins, including the long, thin, handleless French kind I prefer; a pastry pin that is tapered at the ends; a very heavy professional baker's pin; and a nonstick version. Parchment paper and a trifle bowl are also available. Their crystallized ginger, various flours including bread and cake, vanilla extract, and ground cocoa are all excellent.

The catalogue has at least one gingerbread house mold each Christmas. In the past they've sold a heavy iron plaque with a barn on one side and barnyard animals on the other, and one with a Victorian house on one side and a log cabin on the reverse. Other Christmas-appropriate items are a set of six different size heart-shaped cookie cutters; sets of Christmas-themed cutters; male and female gingerbread cookie cutters almost 8″ tall; a Viennese glass cookie stamp; a Tannenbaum plaque, on which star-shaped cookies can be stacked to form a "Christmas tree"; and a Christmas tree cake mold. Contact: Williams-Sonoma, P.O. Box 7456, San Francisco, CA 94120-7456; (415) 421-4242. There are also retail outlets throughout the country.

**COLONIAL GARDENS KITCHENS** offers a much smaller catalogue than the others, but it's often a source for good bargains. In the past, it has had excellent prices on cookie stamps, a square cake pan with a removable bottom, baking parchment, the Cushion-Aire pans, and trifle bowls. Contact: Colonial Gardens Kitchens, Hanover, PA 17333-0066; (800) 752-5552.

The following companies specialize in Christmas cookie molds:

**HOBI HANDCRAFTS:** Gene Wilson's catalogue ($1, refundable with your first order) includes a hundred different molds that he hand-carves. They are all his original designs, but some are based on traditional patterns. They range from small cookie stamps to a 5½″-x-8″ springerle board with twelve pictures representing the twelve days of Christmas. For very reasonable prices, he also fills custom orders—company logos or variations on his other molds—if he feels he can do them justice. Contact: Hobi Handcrafts, P.O. Box 25, Belleville, IL 62222; (618) 233-7689.

**HOUSE-ON-THE-HILL:** This company carries twelve different nickel-plated cherrywood springerle molds and twenty less-expensive ones made from gypsum, a claylike material. They are all traditional designs, often reproduced from museum pieces. Those perfect for Christmas include Nativity scenes, a holiday celebration with dancing couples, and angels. There are also a few Old Testament molds. Each picture is surrounded with an oval or square frame, which makes it look like a lovely, elegant, old-fashioned cameo. Their catalogue is available for $1, refundable with your first purchase. Please write rather than call. Contact: House-on-the-Hill, P.O. Box 221, River Forest, IL 60305.

**MARIA LAXA:**    Mrs. Laxa sells lebkuchen, springerle, or perniky (from her native Czechoslovakia) molds in usable plastic or just decorative hand-painted artstone, all of which are based on designs that date back four hundred years. They are all very reasonably priced. The plastic molds, which come in all sizes, can also be used for marzipan or chocolates. Many of the designs are quite elaborate and beautiful; they include a deer chased by a hound, flowers, men on horseback, angels, and lots of different hearts. Her catalogue costs $3, refundable with your first purchase, and I strongly urge you to look at it. Contact: Maria Laxa, P.O. Box 76, Belmont, MA 02178; (617) 484-0420.

**COOKIES NEWSLETTER:**    For those serious about their cookies, both bakers and collectors of cutters and molds, I recommend a newsletter called *Cookies*. A one-year subscription (six issues) costs $7 and is well worth the price. Contact: *Cookies*, 5426 27th Street, Washington, DC 20015.

**STAMPABARBARA**    is so much fun it seems a pity to mail-order from them rather than stopping by. Unfortunately, they're located only in Santa Barbara and Los Angeles. This rubber stamp store has thousands of stamps, depicting everything from James Dean to invitations to the architectural elements I used in my gingerbread house. Because they are constantly receiving new stamps, there is no catalogue. But, according to owner Gary Dorsey, if you write or call and let them know what you want and in what size, they will send it to you. If you don't like it, it's exchangeable if unused. I love their Tiffany-style windows and doors and the abstract patterns that look like cinder blocks. They can also create stamps to your specifications at very reasonable prices beginning at $10.95. If you're planning to make more than a couple of gingerbread houses over the years, a few rubber stamps (perhaps one door, one window, and one decorative pattern) would be a worthwhile investment. Contact: Studio 15, El Paseo, 813 Anacapa Street, Santa Barbara, CA 93101; (805) 962-4077.

# BIBLIOGRAPHY

The Africa News Service, Inc. *The Africa News Cookbook: African Cooking for Western Kitchens*. New York: Penguin Books, 1985.

Akerstrom, Jenny. *The Swedish Princesses Cook Book*. New York: Albert Bonnier Publishing House, 1936.

Bailey, Adrian, and the Editors of Time-Life Books. *The Cooking of the British Isles*. Alexandria, Va.: Time-Life Books, 1969 (revised 1980).

Beard, James. *Beard on Bread*. New York: Alfred A. Knopf, 1980.

Beer, Gretel. *Austrian Cooking and Baking*. New York: Dover Publications, 1975.

Beeton, Mrs. Isabella. *The Book of Household Management*. London: Ward, Lock, 1899.

Benghiat, Norma. *Traditional Jamaican Cookery*. Harmondsworth, England: Penguin Books, 1985.

Beranbaum, Rose Levy. *The Cake Bible*. New York: William Morrow and Co., 1988.

*Betty Crocker's Baking Classics*. New York: Random House, 1979.

Borgstrom, Greta, and Birgit Danfors. *Scandinavian Cookbook*. Goteborg, Sweden: Wezata Forlag, 1965.

The Boston Cooking School Magazine Co. *American Cookery*, May 1939; June–July 1939.

Boyd, Lizzie, ed. *British Cookery*. London: Croom Helm, 1977.

Břízová, Joza, and Maryna Klimentová. *Czech Cuisine*. Prague: Avicenum, Czechoslovak Medical Press, 1986.

Brobek, Florence, and Monika Kjellberg. *Smorgasbord and Scandinavian Cookery*. New York: Grosset & Dunlap, 1948.

Brown, Cora, Rose, and Bob. *America Cooks*. Garden City, N.Y.: Garden City Books, 1940.

———. *The South American Cook Book*. New York: Dover Publications, 1971.

Brown, Dale, and the Editors of Time-Life Books. *The Cooking of Scandinavia*. Alexandria, Va.: Time-Life Books, 1968 (revised 1977).

———. *American Cooking: The Northwest*. New York: Time-Life Books, 1970.

Brown, Edward Espe. *The Tassajara Bread Book*. Boulder, Co.: Shambhala Publications, 1970.

Cagner, Ewert, comp. *Swedish Christmas*. New York: Henry Holt & Co., n.d.

Child, Julia, and Simone Beck. *Mastering the Art of French Cooking, Vol. 2*. New York: Alfred A. Knopf, 1983.

Claiborne, Craig, with Pierre Franey. *The New New York Times Cookbook*. New York: Times Books, 1979.

Clark, E. Phyllis. *West Indian Cookery*. Edinburgh: Thomas Nelson and Sons/The Government of Trinidad and Tobago, 1945.

Coetzee, Renata. *The South African Culinary Tradition*. Cape Town: C. Struik Publishers, 1977.

*Cooking Magic Step-by-Step Cookbooks*. Chicago: Culinary Arts Institute, 1941–56.

Coombs, Anna Olsson. *The Smorgasbord Cookbook*. New York: A. A. Wyn, 1949.

Craig, Elizabeth. *Court Favorites: Recipes from Royal Kitchens*. London: Andre Deutsch, 1953.

*Creole Recipes*. Photocopied manuscript, n.d.

*Culinary Art and Traditions of Switzerland*. Vevey, Switzerland: Nestlé Products Co., 1987.

Dauzvardis, Josephine J., ed. *Popular Lithuanian Recipes*. Chicago: Lith. Cath. Pres. Society, 1974.

David, Elizabeth. *English Bread and Yeast Cookery*. New York: Viking Press, 1980.

———. *Spices, Salt and Aromatics in the English Kitchen*. Harmondsworth, England: Penguin Books, 1970.

DeWit, Antoinette, and Anita Borghese. *The Complete Book of Indonesian Cooking*. Indianapolis/New York: Bobbs-Merrill, 1973.

Digby, Joan and John, eds. *Food for Thought*. New York: William Morrow and Co., 1987.

Dunnett, Fiona, and Aileen King. *The Home Book of Scottish Cookery*. London: Faber and Faber, 1973.

Exenberger, Maria, and Fritz Breit, comps. *Cookbook from Tyrol*. Soll/Tyrol: Enthaler Verlag, 1982.

Feibleman, Peter S., and the Editors of Time-Life Books. *American Cooking: Creole and Acadian*. New York: Time-Life Books, 1971.

Freeman, Bobby. *First Catch Your Peacock: A Book of Welsh Food*. Griffithstown, Wales: Image Imprint, 1980.

Fussell, Betty. *I Hear America Cooking*. New York: Elisabeth Sifton Books/Viking, 1986.

Gaertner, Pierre, and Robert Frederick. *The Cuisine of Alsace*. Woodbury, N.Y.: Barron's, 1979.

Gardnier, Kenneth. *Creole Caribbean Cookery*. London: Grafton Books, 1986.

Ghanoonparvar, M. R. *Persian Cuisine, Book Two: Regional and Modern Foods*. Lexington, Ky.: Mazda Publishers, 1984.

Gordon, Enid, and Midge Shirley. *The Belgian Cookbook*. London/Sydney: MacDonald & Co., 1982.

Ham, Marion N., and Lynn Ringwald. *Gifts from a Country Kitchen*. New York: Allen D. Bragdon Books, 1984.

Hartley, Dorothy. *Food in England*. London: Futura Publications, 1985.

Hartwig, Daphne Metaxis. *Make Your Own Groceries*. Indianapolis/New York: Bobbs-Merrill, 1979.

Harvey, Irene. *The Jamaican Family Cook Book*. New York: Lore Publishing, 1982.

Hawkins, Nancy and Arthur. *American Regional Cookbook: Recipes from Yesterday and Today for the Modern Cook*. New York: Greenwich House, 1984.

Hazelton, Nika. *American Home Cooking*. New York: Ballantine Books, 1980.

———. *The Belgian Cook Book*. New York: Atheneum, 1985.

Hazelton, Nika Standen, and the Editors of Time-Life Books. *The Cooking of Germany*. Alexandria, Va.: Time-Life Books, 1969 (revised 1977).

Heard, Vida. *Cornish Cookery: Recipes of Today and Yesterday*. Trewolsta, Cornwall: Dyllansow Truran, 1984.

Jadan, Doris and Ivan. *The Virgin Islands Cook House Cook Book*. 1984.

Jadan, Ivan and Christine. *V. I. Cuisine with Ivan and Christine*. U.S. Virgin Islands: Ariel Melchior, Jr., 1979.

Johnny from Holland. *Mama's Favorite Dutch Recipes*. Las Vegas: J.J. Merchandising Co., n.d.

Johnson, Ronald. *The American Table*. New York: Pocket Books, 1986.

Johnston, Mireille. *The Cuisine of the Rose*. New York: Random House, 1982.

Kettilby, Mary. *A Collection of Above Three Hundred Receipts in Cookery, Physick, and Surgery.* London: W. Parker, 1734.

Killeen, Jacqueline, Coralie Castle, and Sharon Silva, eds. *The Whole World Cookbook.* New York: Charles Scribner's Sons, 1979.

Kovi, Paul. *Paul Kovi's Transylvanian Cuisine.* New York: Crown Publishers, 1985.

Krochmal, Connie and Arnold. *Caribbean Cooking.* New York: Quadrangle/New York Times Book Co., 1974.

Ladies Auxiliary of the Hartfield Volunteer Fire Co., comps. *Home Cooking Secrets of Hartfield.* Hartfield, N.Y., n.d.

Ladies of English Fellowship Church in Quito, comps. *Cooking in Ecuador.* Quito, n.d.

Lang, George. *The Cuisine of Hungary.* New York: Bonanza Books, 1971.

Leonard, Jonathan Norton, and the Editors of Time-Life Books. *American Cooking: New England.* New York: Time-Life Books, 1970 (revised 1971).

———. *American Cooking: The Great West.* New York: Time-Life Books, 1971 (revised 1972).

Marks, Copeland. *False Tongues and Sunday Bread.* New York: M. Evans and Co., 1985.

Marshall, Brenda. *The Charles Dickens Cookbook.* Toronto: Personal Library, 1980.

Martin, Pat, comp. *The Czech Book: Recipes and Traditions.* Iowa City: Penfield Press, 1981.

McKendry, Maxime. *The Seven Centuries Cookbook: From Richard II to Elizabeth II.* New York: McGraw-Hill, 1973.

Mickler, Ernest Matthew. *White Trash Cooking.* Berkeley: Ten Speed Press, 1986.

Moncure, Blanche Elbert. *Emma Jane's Souvenir Cook Book.* Williamsburg, Va., 1937.

Neal, Bill. *Bill Neal's Southern Cooking.* Chapel Hill: University of North Carolina Press, 1985.

Newman, Graeme. *The Down Under Cookbook: An Authentic Guide to Australian Cooking and Eating Traditions.* New York: Harrow and Heston, 1987.

*Oetker German Home Cooking.* Bielefeld, Germany: Ceres-Verlag Rudolf-August Oetker KG, 1963.

Ojakangas, Beatrice. *The Finnish Cook Book.* New York: Crown Publishers, 1964.

Ojakangas, Beatrice, John Zug, and Sue Roemig. *Fantastically Finnish: Recipes and Traditions.* Iowa City: Penfield Press, 1985.

Ortiz, Elisabeth Lambert. *The Complete Book of Caribbean Cooking.* New York: M. Evans and Co., 1973.

Ostmann, Barbara Gibbs, and Jane Baker, eds. *Food Editors' Hometown Favorites.* Maplewood, N.J.: Hammond Inc., 1984.

Papashvily, Helen and George, and the Editors of Time-Life Books. *Russian Cooking.* Alexandria, Va.: Time-Life Books, 1969 (revised 1977).

*The Picayune Creole Cook Book.* New York: Dover Publications, 1971.

Polvay, Marina. *The Dracula Cookbook.* New York: Chelsea House Publishers, 1978.

*Restaurants of Jamaica, 1985–1986.* Montego Bay: The Restaurant Guide for Jamaica, 1985.

Roalson, Louise. *Notably Norwegian.* Iowa City: Penfield Press, 1982.

Roate, Mettja Cappon. *The New Hamburger and Hot Dog Cookbook.* New Rochelle, N.Y.: Arlington House, 1975.

Rombauer, Irma S., and Marion Rombauer Becker. *Joy of Cooking*. Indianapolis/New York: Bobbs-Merrill, 1975.

Root, Waverly. *Food*. New York: Simon & Schuster, 1980.

Rosenblatt, Julia Carlson, and Frederic H. Sonnenschmidt. *Dining with Sherlock Holmes*. Indianapolis/New York: Bobbs-Merrill, 1976.

Rosicky, Mary. *Bohemian-American Cook Book*. Omaha: National Printing Co., 1915.

Sanson, William. *A Book of Christmas*. New York: McGraw-Hill, 1968.

*Scandinavian Christmas: Recipes and Traditions*. Iowa City: Penfield Press, 1982.

Shenton, James P., Angelo M. Pellegrini, Dale Brown, Israel Shenker, Peter Wood, and the Editors of Time-Life Books. *American Cooking: The Melting Pot*. New York: Time-Life Books, 1971 (revised 1972).

Sheraton, Mimi. *The German Cookbook*. New York: Random House, 1965.

Shibles, Loana, and Annie Rogers, eds. *Maine Cookery Then and Now*. Rockland: Courier-Gazette, 1972.

Silitch, Clarissa M., ed. *The Old Farmer's Almanac Colonial Cookbook*. Dublin, N.H.: Yankee Books, 1976.

Smith, Gunilla, ed. *Scandinavian Cooking*. New York: Crown Publishers, 1976.

Solum, Pat. *Danish Cook Book*. Big Bear Lake, Ca., n.d.

Spence, Wenton O. *Jamaican Cookery: Recipes from Old Jamaican Grandmothers*. Kingston: Heritage Publishers, 1981.

Stamm, Sara B. B., and the Editors of *Yankee* Magazine. *Yankee Magazine's Favorite New England Recipes*. Dublin, N.H.: Yankee Books, 1979.

Standard, Stella. *Our Daily Bread*. New York: Funk & Wagnalls, 1970.

Stern, Jane and Michael. *Roadfood and Goodfood*. New York: Alfred A. Knopf, 1986.

The Editors of Sunset Books and *Sunset* Magazine. *Sunset Scandinavian Cook Book*. Menlo Park, Ca.: Lane Publishing, 1974.

Thompson, Martha Wiberg. *Superbly Swedish: Recipes and Traditions*. Iowa City: Penfield Press, 1983.

Tri-Vingfa (Virgin Islands National Guard Family Auxiliary). *Traditional and Contemporary Virgin Islands Cooking*. U.S. Virgin Islands: Tri-Vingfa, 1986.

Van Klompenburg, Carol. *Delightfully Dutch: Recipes and Traditions*. Iowa City: Penfield Press, 1984.

Wason, Betty. *The Art of German Cooking*. Garden City, N.Y.: Doubleday, 1967.

Wechsberg, Joseph, and the Editors of Time-Life Books. *The Cooking of Vienna's Empire*. New York: Time-Life Books, 1974.

Wilson, C. Anne. *Food and Drink in Britain: From the Stone Age to Recent Times*. Harmondsworth, England: Penguin Books, 1984.

Wilson, Jose, and the Editors of Time-Life Books. *American Cooking: The Eastern Heartland*. Alexandria, Va.: Time-Life Books, 1971 (revised 1977).

Witty, Helen, and Elizabeth Schneider Colchie. *Better Than Store-Bought*. New York: Harper & Row, 1979.

Wolcott, Imogene. *The New England Yankee Cookbook*. New York: Coward-McCann, 1939.

Ykema-Steenbergen, Rie. *The Real Dutch Treat Cook Book*. Grand Rapids, Mi.: William B. Eerdmans, 1949.

Page numbers in italics indicate recipes.

aachener, 165
aegte Danske klejner, 35
Africa, 9, 21, 49
ale, in parkin, 15
almond, 15, 104, 163
 cake, 13, *65*, *72*
 cookies, *20–21*, *28*, *43–44*, *60*,
  *83*, *104*
 frangipane tarts, *88*
 marzipan, 17, *167*, *183*
 tortoni, *104*
amaretti, *104*
ammonium carbonate, 14, 166, 181
apple (see also cider, boiled)
 baked, *44*, *82*, *85*, *152*
 bread pudding, *106*
 brown betty, *95*
 cake, 49, *53*, *64*, 163
 dumplings, *90*
 mincemeat, *150*
 pancakes/blintzes, *132*, *134*
applesauce, 49, *52*, *60*, *142*
apricot, *150*, *167*
 cookies, *36*, *46*
 glaze, *53*
Asia, 9–10, 16, *68*, 116, 141, *158*
Austria, 9, 20, *90*

bacon (see also spekkoek), *96*, *144*,
 *154*
 and cabbage strudel, *152*
baked Alaska, *66*
baked apples (see apple, baked)
baking powder/soda, 15, 166
banana, 49, *70*, *86*
 cupcakes/muffins, *80*, *126*
 exotic, where to buy, 80
 fritters, *96*
banana bread, *126*
 bread pudding, *106*
beef, 117, 141
 meatloaf, *154*
 mincemeat-stuffed peppers,
  *150*
 sauerbraten, 10, 141, *142*
 tostadas, *134*, 141, *156*
beer, 15, *60*
Beeton, Mrs. Isabella, 150
Belgium, 111, 162, 165

berry (see also each berry)
 shortcake, *120*
 tacos, *83*
 -topped cake, *55*, *65*, *72*, *74*
biscotti, *28*
biscuits, *120*
blackberry tarts, *88*
black bun, 162, 164
black cake, 162, 163
blintzes, *134*, 141, *156*
blueberry, *88*, 133
 blintzes, *134*
bow ties, *35*
bran, 13
 muffins, *127*
brandy, 15, 20, 22, *32*, *150*, 162–
 163, *167*
 sauce, *48*
bread (see also specific names), 9,
 13, 52, 111, *112–137*, 141, 163
 pudding, *106*
 quick, *116–117*, *120–121*, *126–
 127*
 rising technique, 112
 storage, 111
 sweet, *118*, 163
 yeast, *112–114*, *118*, *122–124*,
  *137*, *146*, *154*
breadfruit, 49
brioches, *104*, *106*, *118*, *127*, *137*
Britain, 10, 14, 16–17, 20, *25*, *30*,
 *44*, *47*, 49, *60*, *121*, 132, 144,
 162–165, *167*
broccoli stuffing, *148*
brown betty, *95*, *152*
Brown, Edward Espe, 111
brownies, *48*, *99*
bundt cake, *58*
buttermilk, 15, 49, 60
 pancakes/waffles, *131*, *133*
 biscuits, *120*
 kringles, *34*
butterscotch chips, 10, *42*, *47*, *80*
butterscotch sauce, *48*, *52*

cabbage, 141–142
 and bacon strudel, *152*
cake (see also torte; specific
 names), 9, 49–51, *52–81*

coffee, topping, *107*
 jellyroll-type, 50, *55*, *180*
 layer, 50, 51, *62*, *65*, *70*
 mail order supplies, 179–182
 spice proportions, 13, 51
 tube (ring), *58*, *61*, *162*
canapes, *114*, *117*, *128*, *157*
cannoli, 10, *82*, *102–103*, *181*
caramel toppings, *32*, *48*, *55*, *57*, *74*,
 *98*, *133*
Caribbean, 9, 12, 15, 17, *21*, 49, 96,
 126, 130, 162–164, *167*
carp, 141, 162–164
carrots, 49, *154*
checkerboard cake, 50, *62*, *181*
cheese, 116, 132, 136, 144, *158*
 and tomato croutes, *117*, *157*
 blintzes, *134*
 strudel, *152*
 tostadas, *156*
cheesecake, *40*, *51*, *107*, *128*
 gingerbread swirl, 10, *75*
 vanilla "Swiss walnut," *77*
chicken, stuffed, *116*, 141, *146*
chicken tostadas, *134*, 141, *156*
chocolate, 15, 40, 181, 183
 brownies, *48*
 -chip cookies/bars, *41*, *47*
 -chip cannoli filling, *102*
 -chunk waffles, *133*
 cookie roll, *21*
 -covered cookies, *28*, *38*
 -covered nuts cheesecake,
  *77*
 cream filling, *86–87*, *98*
 frosting/glaze, *65*, *70*
 -ginger madeleines, *40*
 ice cream, *32*, *66*, *99*
 layer cake, 10, *68*, *167*
 mousse, *83*
 nut torte, *72*
 sauce, *72*, *98*
 truffles, *97*
chocolate, white, torte, 10, *74*
Christmas, 49, 141, 161, 179–183
 cake, 111, 161–164, *167*, *181*
 cookies, 20, *23*, 161–165, *166*,
  179–183
 edible ornaments, *23*, 162, *166*

cider, boiled
  and apple pie, *92–93*
  honey, *92–93, 130, 133,* 137
cinnamon sugar, *137, 165*
citron, candied, 20, *167*
cobbler's pancakes, *132,* 182
coconut, 15, *80, 130*
  cake with mocha frosting, *70*
  cookies, *27*
  flakes, toasted, *27, 70*
coffee, 15, 17, *55,* 58, *72,* 96, *97,*
    163
  frosting/filling, *71, 87*
  ice cream, 62
cognac (*see* brandy)
cookies (*see also* specific names), 9,
    20–22, *23–48,* 141
  bar, 21, *47–48,* 162, 165
  bowls, *32, 43*
  coloring, 165, 171, 172, 180
  mail order supplies, 180–183
  molded, about, 9, 16–17, 20–22,
    *31, 40, 43, 162–165*
  molds/stamps, 11, 40, 164, 169,
    179, 180–183
  newsletter, 183
  printed/stamped, 11, 20, 164,
    165, *169, 171*
  spice proportions, 13, 21
  storage, 22, 23, 38, 170, 171
  texture, 13, 21, 22
corn, 141
  dogs, 136, *149*
  hush puppies, 131, *136*
  pancakes, *131*
  bread/sticks/muffins, *116,* 141
  bread stuffing, *146*
Cornish pasties, 144
cornstarch, 13, *30*
crab stuffing, *148*
cream, about, 15
cream cheese (*see also* cheesecake),
    97, 128
  pastry, *36*
cream puffs, 82, 98
cream, sour, 15, 49, *58, 121*
cream, whipped, 15, *21, 25,* 50
  -topping, *48,* 49–50, *52, 55, 65,*
    *74, 83, 86–88, 91, 98, 120, 133*
creme anglaise, *91*
creme fraiche, *52*

crinkles, 21
Crocker, Betty, 90
croquettes, potato, 10, 154, *158*
croutes, tomato/cheese, 117, *157*
crunchy nut topping, *107*
cupcakes, banana, *80,* 126
cupcakes, candied ginger, *79*
curry, 141, 158
Czechoslovakia, 21, 49, *90,* 163,
    183

Dickinson, Emily, 17
deep-fried cookies, 35
Dominica cake, 162, 163
doughnuts, potato, *100*
dumplings, *90,* 142

eggs, about, 15
empanadas, *144*
equipment, baking, 11, 50–51, 165,
    169, 179–183
estomac mulatre, 17
Europe (*see also* each country), 13,
    16–17, 20, *46,* 50, *72,* 141, *152,*
    164

fats, about, 14, 49
fattigmand, 35, *181*
fig cake, *60, 167*
filling (*see also* stuffing)
  chocolate cream, *86–87,* 98
  ricotta, 10, *98, 102–103*
fish, 96, 136, 141, *148, 162–164*
fladli, 35
flour, about, 13, 49, *181*
fortune cookies, 22, *45*
France, 9, 16, *43, 65,* 111, *118,* 163,
    164
frangipane tarts, *88*
French toast, *137*
fritters, 131
  banana, *96*
frosting (*see also* specific names),
    49, 51, *62–63, 66–67, 70–71,*
    *181*
fruit (*see also* specific fruits), 15,
    49, 82, 96, 126, 133
  bread, 111, 162–163
  dumplings, *90*
  pastries, *86, 88, 152*
  sauce, *61*

fruit, candied (*see also* specific
    fruits), *60, 167*
fruit, dried (*see also* fruitcake;
    raisins), *36, 150*
fruitcake, 162–164, *167*
Fussell, Betty, 41

genoise cake, 65
Germany, 9–10, 14, 16, 20, *35, 90,*
    111, 141, *142, 152, 162–165*
ginger, 9, 12, 16, 164–165
  combinations, 15, 21, 34, 40, 51,
    *96, 97,* 111, *131,* 141
  juice, *12*
  medical effects of, 10, 26
  nuts, 21
  rolls, *124*
ginger, candied, 12, *181*
  cake/cupcakes, *53, 79, 167*
  chocolate truffles, *97*
  cookies, 20, *28*
  crunchy nut topping, *107*
  filling, 10, *98, 102–103*
ginger, fresh, 12
  and banana, *80,* 126
  and chocolate, *48, 72*
  corn bread stuffing, *146*
  orange-buttermilk waffles, *133*
gingerbread
  cake, basic, 9, 51, *52,* 64
  checkerboard cake, 50, *62,* 181
  cheesecake swirl, 10, *75*
  -chunk ice cream, *99*
  crumbs in sauce, 10, *85,* 141, *142,*
    *163–164*
  definition and taste of, 9
  history, 9–10, 14, 16–17, *52, 60,*
    111, 164
  husbands, 17
  -ice cream cake roll, *55*
  men, 16, *23,* 163, *166, 173, 181*
gingerbread house, *23,* 162, *166,*
    *169–173, 180–183*
gingersnaps, 10, 20–21, *25,* 44, 82,
    141, 162, 166
  brown betty, *95*
  chocolate nut torte, *72*
  -chunk ice cream, *99*
  coating, 10, *97,* 154, *158*
  crunchy nut topping, *107*
  crust, 10, *77, 82, 92–94*

mincemeat, *150*
meatloaf, *154*
sauce, 10, 141, *142*, 163–164
strudel, *152*
stuffing, *85*, 148
glaze, 17, *65*, 72, 162, 172
apricot, *53*
for fruit breads, *111*
honey-mustard for chicken, *146*
glogg punch, 49, 163
graham crackers, 13, *128*, 141
baked apple stuffing, 82, *85*
chocolate torte, *72*
crust, *77*, *82*, *93–94*
meatloaf, *154*
graham flour, 13
grybai, 20
Guatemala, 21

ham, 120, 131, 141, *146*, *148*
hard sauce, *52*, *106*
hartshorn, powdered, 14
hazelnut, *133*
chocolate torte, 13, *72*
cookies, 20, *28*
hermits, 21
honey, 13–14, 16, 20, 22, 92, 111, 162, 164–165
bread, *112–116*, *118–120*, *122*
cake, *52*, *66*, 163–164
cookies, *31*, *43*, *45*, *47–48*, *83*
crunchy nut topping, *107*
cupcakes, *79*
graham crackers, *128*
hush puppies, *136*
pancakes, *131*
-mustard glaze, *146*
hot dogs, *136*, *149*
hush puppies, 131, *136*, *149*
hussar balls, *46*

ice cream, 40, *82*, 77, *107*
as filling, *32*, *43*, *86*, *98*
as topping, *48–49*, *52*, *61*, 95, *133*
cake, *55*, *66*
gingerbread chunk, *99*
praline, *32*, *57*
sundae, *48*
icing (*see* frosting)

ingredients, about, 12–15, 20, 52, 179–181
Italy, 16, *28*, *35*, 82, *102*

jalapeño corn bread, *116*
jam, 46, 50, 121
jelly, 112, 121
-roll-type cake, 50, *55*, 180
Jewish, 36
Joe Froggers, 21

krapfen, 35
kringles, *34*

lace cookies, *32*
Latin America, 116, *156*, *158*
leavening, about, 9, 14, 166
lebkuchen, 14, 20, 162–163, 165, 181, 183
leek stuffing, 146–148
lemon, 15, 40, *106*, *150*
cake, 50, *52*, *62*, *167*
icing/frosting, 49, *70*, *111*
sauce, 49, *52*
licorice gingerbread, 17
liqueur, 15, *94–95*, *104*, 162
cake, *72*, 162–163, *167*
and chocolate, *87*, *97*
mincemeat, *150*
tortoni, *104*
liquids, about, 15
Lithuania, 20

macaroons, 14, 20, *44*, *104*, 165
crunchy topping, *58*, *107*
stuffing, *85*, *148*
mail ordering, 11, 80, 179–183
maple syrup, *130*, *133*, *137*
meatloaf, *154*, *158*
meringue, 14, *62–63*, *66–67*
Middle East, 16, 157
milk, about, 15, 49, 111
mincemeat-stuffed peppers, *150*
mint cookies, *40*
mocha frosting, *70–71*
molasses, 9, 13–17, 20, 22, 79, 111, 162
bread, 111, *112–114*, *117–118*, *122–124*
cake, *52–64*, *66*, *70–72*, *75*, *167*

cookies, 20–21, *23–27*, *32*, *36–41*, *43*, *47–48*, 83, *170*
-corn batters, *136*, *149*
fruit dessert, *83*, *90*, *95*, *134*
graham crackers, *128*
muffins, *127*
pancakes/waffles, *130–135*
pastry, *83*, *86*, *98*, *100*, *124*, *145*
Moravian ginger cookies, 21, 163
Mothering Sunday wafers, 20
mousse, *83*, *86*, *107*
muffins, 107, 111
banana, *126*
bran, *127*
corn, *116*
mushroom, 20, *146*, *152*
crab-stuffed, *148*
mustard, *136*, *149*
-honey glaze, *146*
muster gingerbread, 17

Netherlands, 10, 16, 20, *68*, *132*, 162, 165
New Year's Eve, 162, 164
nuts (*see* specific names)

oatmeal, 21, 51
cake, 10, 13, 15, 51, *60*
cookies, 13, 15, 20, 26, 60
oil, olive, about, 157
Olney, Judith, 40
onion, 131, *142–144*, *152–156*
-walnut bread, 10, *117*, 157
Onufrychuk, Brian, 42
orange, 15, 20, *52*, *87*, *94–95*, *106*, *137*, *150*, 163, 181
-buttermilk waffles, *133*
cake, *72*, *167*
candied, *167*

pain d'epices, 9, 111
pancakes, *130*, 142
apple/cobbler's, *132*, *134*, 180
blintzes/crepes, *134*, 141, *156*
corn, *131*
parkin, 10, 15, 20, *60*
pastry (*see also* piecrust; specific names), 9, 14, 82, 141
cream, *88*
peach, *55*, *64–65*, *167*

peanut butter, 112
  cookies, 10, *42*
pear, *36, 64, 95*, 111, *134, 162, 167*
  brown betty, *106, 152*
pebbernodder, 162
pecan, *133*
  cake/cupcakes, *58, 79–80, 167*
  cookies, 42, *46–47*
  crunchy nut topping, *107*
  custard pie, 10, *93, 94*
pepparkakor, 22, 163, *166*
peppers, 154
  stuffed, *150*
perniky, 183
pie (see *also* quiche, sausage), 82,
    86, *144*
  cider and apple, *92–93*
  pecan custard, 10, *93–94*
piecrust
  cream cheese, *36*
  ginger crumb, 10, 82, *92–94, 128*
  pastry, *144–145*
  tart shells, *86–88, 150*
pineapple upside-down cake, *64*
pistachio cookies, *21*
pits of love, *46*
plantain cake, 49
Poland, 163
pork (see *also* bacon; ham), 14, 96,
    131
  tostadas, 141, *156*
Portugal, 16
potato, *124, 142*, 154
  cake, 49, *58*
  croquettes, 10, 154, *158*
  doughnuts, *100*
potato bread (see *also* brioches;
    whole wheat bread), 111, *112*
  crumbs, meatloaf, *154*
  French toast, *137*
  poultry stuffing, *146*
  bread pudding, *106*
  zweiback, *122*
pound cake, *40, 61, 163*
praline ice cream, *32, 57*
praline sauce, *91*
preserves (see *also* specific fruits),
    *61, 121, 130, 167*
printen, 165
profiteroles, *98*
prune butter, 50

pudding, *61, 82, 107*
  bread, *106*
pumpkin, 49

quiche, sausage, *144*

rabbit, jugged, 141
raisins, *26, 36, 88, 90, 106, 124,
    167*, 141, *150*
raspberry jam cookies, *46*
rhubarb, 49
rice flour, 13, *30*
rice paper, 44
ricotta filling, 10, *98, 102–103*
rolled cookies, *20–22, 23–25, 99*
  as sauce thickener, 141, *142*
rolls, ginger, *124*
rugelach cookies, *36*
rum, 15, 21, *162–163*
  sauce, *48*
Russia, 9, 164
rye flour, 13, 20, *52*

salsa, *156*
sand tarts, *31, 180*
sandalwood, 17
sandwich cookies, *38*
sauce (see specific names)
sauerbraten, 10, 1**4**1, *142*
sauerkraut, *142*
sausage, *116, 136, 142, 149*
  quiche, *144*
savory dishes, 111, *112, 137*, 139–
    141, *142–159*
Scandinavia, 9, 13, 20, *31, 34–35,
    49, 162–163, 166*
scones, *121*
Shah biscuits, 20
shortbread, 13, *30, 31, 34*, 180
shortcake, *65, 120*
shrimp-stuffed mushrooms, *148*
soup, 12, 126, 128, 141, 152
soursop, 49
speculaas, *162*, 165
spekkoek, 10, *68*
spekulatius, Rhineland, 165
spice, *12–13, 16–17, 20*, 111, *132,*
    164
  bread (see *also* pain d'epices),
    111, *162–163*
  cake, 9, *162–164, 167*

cookies, 20, *162–165*
  proportions, 13, 21, 51
springerle, 165, *180, 181, 182, 183*
strawberry, *65, 83, 88, 134*
  ice cream, *66*
  jam or preserves cookies, *46*
  mousse, *83*
  sauce, *104*
streusel mixture, *107*
strubli, 35
strudel, cabbage and bacon, *152*
stuffing (see *also* filling)
  corn bread, *116*, 141, *146*
stuffed baked apple, 44, 82, *85*
stuffed mushrooms, *148*
stuffed peppers, *150*
sugar, 14, *16–17, 22, 25, 36*, 44, 61,
    97, 181
  topping, *58, 64*, 111, *124, 133–
    134, 137, 164, 165*
sweeteners (see *also* specific
    names), 9, *12–14, 16, 49, 92–
    93*
sweet potato, 49
Switzerland, 49, 111, *162, 163, 164*
syrup, *13–14, 21, 130, 133, 137*

taco, 43, 52, 82, 83, *156*
tangerine rind fruitcake, *167*
tartlets
  chocolate-filled, *86–87*
  shells, *86–88, 150*
  tins, *88, 104, 127*
tarts, 82
  frangipane, *88*
  fruit, *86–88*
  mincemeat, *150*
tea, 9, 17, 164
thumbprint cookies, *46*
tollhouse cookies, 41
tomato, *156*
  sauce, *150*
  sun-dried, croutes, *117, 157*
tongue in raisin sauce, 141
topping (see *also* specific recipes),
    49, 52, *130, 137*
  crunchy nut, *107*
torte, 13, 51, 163
  chocolate nut, *72*
  white chocolate, 10, *74*
tortoni, *104*

tostadas, *134, 141, 156*
treacle, 14, 17, *60*
trifle, 44, 61, 181, 182
truffles, chocolate, *97*
tuiles, *22, 43, 83*
twelfth cake, 162, 163, 164

United States, 10, 13–14, 17, 21, *25, 49–50, 52–53, 83, 90, 100–102, 116, 126, 131, 132, 157, 158, 162–164, 167*
upside-down cake, *64*

Valentine's Day, 165
vanilla, *15, 40, 70,* 181
ice cream, *32, 55, 57, 66, 77, 95, 99, 133*
Swiss walnut cheesecake, *77*

vegetable batters, 15, 49
venison in ginger sauce, 141
vinegar (*see also* sauerbraten), 15, *25, 27,* 142

waffles, orange-buttermilk, *133*
walnut, *133*
cake, 13, *58, 72, 74, 167*
chocolate, in cheesecake, *77*
cookies, 21, *36, 42, 46–48*
cupcakes, *79–80*
-onion bread, 10, *117, 157*
stuffing/topping, *85, 107, 124*
water chestnut stuffing, *146–148*
wedding cake, *167,* 180
white icing, 111, 165, *170*

whole wheat (*see also* graham crackers), 13
bran muffins, 127
cake, *52, 58*
corn batter, *136, 149*
crunchy nut topping, *107*
ginger rolls, *124*
whole wheat bread, 13, *114,* 154
French toast, *137*
onion-walnut, *117*
poultry stuffing, *146*
bread pudding, *106*
wine dough, 17, *102*
Wright, Frank Lloyd, 169

yogurt, 15, 126

zweiback, *122*